Math and Literature
Grades 6-8

Math and Literature
Grades 6–8

Jennifer M. Bay-Williams
Sherri L. Martinie

Introduction by

Marilyn Burns

Math Solutions
Sausalito, California, USA

Math Solutions
One Harbor Drive, Suite 101
Sausalito, California, USA 94965
www.mathsolutions.com

Library of Congress Cataloging-in-Publication Data
Bay-Williams, Jennifer M.
  Math and literature. Grades 6–8 / Jennifer M. Bay-Williams, Sherri L. Martinie.
    p.   cm.
 Includes bibliographical references and index.
   ISBN 0-941355-63-2 (alk. paper)
  1. Mathematics—Study and teaching (Middle school)   2. Children's literature in mathematics education.   I. Martinie, Sherri L.   II. Title.
   QA135.6.B39 2004
    372.7—dc22

                                                                                2004010069

ISBN-13: 978-0-941355-63-6

Math Solutions is a division of Houghton Mifflin Harcourt.

Editor: Toby Gordon
Production: Melissa L. Inglis
Cover and interior design: Catherine Hawkes/Cat and Mouse
Composition: TechBooks

Printed in the United States of America.
8 9 10 11 12   6710   23 22 21 20
4510006884

A Message from Math Solutions

We at Math Solutions believe that teaching math well calls for increasing our understanding of the math we teach, seeking deeper insights into how students learn mathematics, and refining our lessons to best promote students' learning.

Math Solutions shares classroom-tested lessons and teaching expertise from our faculty of professional development consultants as well as from other respected math educators. Our publications are part of the nationwide effort we've made since 1984 that now includes

- more than five hundred face-to-face professional development programs each year for teachers and administrators in districts across the country;
- professional development books that span all math topics taught in kindergarten through high school;
- videos for teachers and for parents that show math lessons taught in actual classrooms;
- on-site visits to schools to help refine teaching strategies and assess student learning; and
- free online support, including grade-level lessons, book reviews, inservice information, and district feedback, all in our Math Solutions Online Newsletter.

For information about all of the products and services we have available, please visit our website at *www.mathsolutions.com*. You can also contact us to discuss math professional development needs by calling (800) 868-9092 or by sending an email to *info@mathsolutions.com*.

We're always eager for your feedback and interested in learning about your particular needs. We look forward to hearing from you.

Contents

Contents

Acknowledgments

We would like to thank the teachers and students who participated in the development and teaching of the activities we share in this book:

students in grades 6 through 8, Wamego Middle School, Wamego, Kansas;

Andrea Fields and her sixth graders, Amanda Arnold Elementary School, Manhattan, Kansas;

Karen Grokett and her sixth graders, Chase County Middle School, Topeka, Kansas;

Lee Anne Coester, Washburn University, who contributed the lesson taught in Karen Grokett's classroom, titled *Shipwreck at the Bottom of the World*;

Melisa Hancock and her fifth and sixth graders, Bluemont Elementary School, Manhattan, Kansas; and

Alisha Yarnall McClure for her assistance in observing and capturing the lessons.

A very special thanks to our families for their support and encouragement throughout the development of this book.

Introduction

For months before publishing this resource of classroom-tested lessons, I was surrounded by children's books. They were stacked practically up to my ears on my desk and additional piles were all around on the floor. It took some fancy shuffling at times to make space for other things that needed my attention. But I never complained. I love children's books and it was pure pleasure to be immersed in reading them and then teaching, writing, revising, and editing lessons that use them as springboards for teaching children mathematics.

This book is one in our new Math Solutions Publications series for teaching mathematics using children's literature, and I'm pleased to present the complete series:

Math and Literature, Grades K–1
Math and Literature, Grades 2–3
Math and Literature, Grades 4–6, Second Edition
Math and Literature, Grades 6–8
Math and Nonfiction, Grades K–2
Math and Nonfiction, Grades 3–5

More than ten years ago we published my book *Math and Literature (K–3)*. My premise for that book was that children's books can be effective vehicles for motivating children to think and reason mathematically. I searched for books that I knew would stimulate children's imaginations and that also could be used to teach important math concepts and skills.

After that first book's publication, my colleague Stephanie Sheffield began sending me the titles of children's books she had discovered and descriptions of the lessons she had taught based on them. Three years after publishing my book, we published Stephanie's *Math and Literature (K–3), Book Two*. And the following year we published

Rusty Bresser's *Math and Literature (Grades 4–6)*, a companion to the existing books.

Over the years, some of the children's books we initially included in our resources have, sadly, gone out of print. However, other wonderful titles have emerged. For this new series, we did a thorough review of our three original resources. Stephanie and I collaborated on substantially revising our two K–3 books and reorganizing them into two different books, one for grades K–1 and the other for grades 2–3. Rusty produced a second edition of his book for grades 4–6.

In response to the feedback we received from teachers, we became interested in creating a book that would offer lessons based on children's books for middle school students, and we were fortunate enough to find two wonderful teachers, Jennifer M. Bay-Williams and Sherri L. Martinie, to collaborate on this project. I'm pleased to present their book, *Math and Literature, Grades 6–8*.

The two books that round out our series use children's nonfiction as springboards for lessons. Jamee Petersen created *Math and Nonfiction, Grades K–2*, and Stephanie Sheffield built on her experience with the Math and Literature books to team with her colleague Kathleen Gallagher to write *Math and Nonfiction, Grades 3–5*. Hearing nonfiction books read aloud to them requires children to listen in a different way than usual. With nonfiction, students listen to the facts presented and assimilate that information into what they already know about that particular subject. And rather than reading from cover to cover as with fiction, it sometimes makes more sense to read only a small portion of a nonfiction book and investigate the subject matter presented in that portion. The authors of these Math and Nonfiction books are sensitive to the demands of nonfiction and how to present new information in order to make it accessible to children.

We're still fond of the lessons that were based on children's books that are now out of print, and we know that through libraries, the Internet, and used bookstores, teachers have access to some of those books. Therefore, we've made all of the older lessons that are not included in the new series of books available online at *www.mathsolutions.com*. Please visit our Web site for those lessons and for additional support for teaching math.

I'm pleased and proud to present these new books. It was a joy to work on them, and I'm convinced that you and your students will benefit from the lessons we offer.

MARILYN BURNS
2004

Contents Chart

	Lessons	Author	Type of Literature	Number	Geometry	Patterns/Algebra	Measurement	Data Analysis/Probability
1	A Drop of Water	Walter Wick	Nonfiction		✔	✔	✔	
2	Earthshine	Theresa Nelson	Young Adult Fiction	✔			✔	
3	Eighteen Flavors	Shel Silverstein	Poem			✔	✔	✔
4	The Greedy Triangle	Marilyn Burns	Children's Fiction		✔	✔		
5	Harry Potter and the Sorcerer's Stone	J. K. Rowling	Young Adult Fiction	✔		✔	✔	✔
6	How Big Is a Foot?	Rolf Myller	Children's Fiction	✔			✔	
7	How Much Is a Million?	David M. Schwartz	Children's Fiction	✔			✔	
8	Jim and the Beanstalk	Raymond Briggs	Children's Fiction	✔			✔	
9	One Inch Tall	Shel Silverstein	Poem	✔			✔	
10	Shapes	Shel Silverstein	Poem	✔			✔	
11	Shipwreck at the Bottom of the World	Jennifer Armstrong	Young Adult Nonfiction	✔			✔	
12	Spaghetti and Meatballs for All!	Marilyn Burns	Children's Fiction	✔		✔	✔	
13	Tikki Tikki Tembo	Arlene Mosel	Children's Fiction					✔
14	What's Faster Than a Speeding Cheetah?	Robert E. Wells	Children's Nonfiction	✔			✔	

	Additional Ideas	Author	Type of Literature	Number	Geometry	Patterns/Algebra	Measurement	Data Analysis/Probability
15	Animal Farm	George Orwell	Young Adult Fiction	✔				
16	Anno's Hat Tricks	Akihiro Nozaki	Children's Fiction					✔
17	Factastic Book of 1,001 Lists	Russell Ash	Young Adult Nonfiction	✔				✔
18	Far North	Will Hobbs	Young Adult Fiction	✔		✔	✔	
19	The 512 Ants on Sullivan Street	Carol Losi	Children's Fiction	✔		✔		
20	Holes	Louis Sachar	Young Adult Fiction		✔		✔	
21	The King's Giraffe	Mary J. Collier and Peter Collier	Children's Nonfiction	✔		✔	✔	
22	The Missing Piece	Shel Silverstein	Children's Fiction	✔	✔		✔	
23	My Little Sister Ate One Hare	Bill Grossman	Children's Fiction	✔				✔
24	One Hundred Hungry Ants	Elinor J. Pinczes	Children's Fiction	✔				
25	The Phantom Tollbooth	Norton Juster	Young Adult Fiction	✔				✔
26	Roll of Thunder, Hear My Cry	Mildred D. Taylor	Young Adult Fiction	✔		✔	✔	
27	The Tell-Tale Heart	Edgar Allen Poe	Young Adult Fiction			✔		
28	The Village of Round and Square Houses	Ann Grifalconi	Children's Nonfiction		✔		✔	
29	What's Smaller Than a Pygmy Shrew?	Robert E. Wells	Children's Nonfiction	✔			✔	
30	Wilma Unlimited	Kathleen Krull	Children's Nonfiction	✔		✔	✔	

Part One

Lessons

A Drop of Water

Walter Wick's short picture book *A Drop of Water* (1997) describes scientific qualities of water. Beautiful photographs show what can happen with soap bubbles when different objects are dipped in soapy water. One photograph shows a bubble that is a perfect sphere.

In this investigation, students use bubble mix to blow bubbles onto their desks. When the bubbles pop, they leave residue in the shape of a circle. Students use the circles to investigate relationships among the radius, diameter, and circumference of circles. This lesson is useful for introducing pi (the relationship between the diameter and the circumference of a circle).

MATERIALS

string, 1 2-foot piece for each student

rulers, 1 per student

containers of bubble mix, 1 per group of four

straws, 1 per student

paper towels

circular objects of various sizes, 1 per group

plastic cups half filled with water, 1 per group of four students

Introducing the Investigation

I began the lesson by asking students what kinds of bubbles they had made in the past. Students shared that they had made bubbles with gum and with bubble mix. After reading *A Drop of Water*, I asked students to each take out a ruler and to clear off their desks completely.

On the board, I had created a large blank four-column table for recording data. I labeled the first column *Circle Number*. I asked students what a diameter of a circle was. Ariella said, "It goes all the way across the circle."

Madison added, "It has to go through the center."

I labeled the second column *Diameter* and then asked the students if they knew what a radius was. Lucas came to the board, drew a circle, and then drew a radius on the circle. I labeled the third column *Radius*.

Finally, I asked for someone to tell me what a circumference was. I labeled the fourth column *Circumference*.

Circle Number	Diameter	Radius	Circumference

I explained to students that today we were going to look at circles made by bubbles. We were going to look at many different-sized circles and measure the diameter, radius, and circumference of each one. In the end, our goal was to find relationships among these measurements. I explained that they were going to have bubble mix and use it to create bubbles on their desks. As with the use of any tool, we discussed what was appropriate use of the materials we were using that day. Students agreed that the only way they would use the bubbles was to make bubbles on their desks for the purpose of measuring them. I removed the blow sticks from the bottles to avoid temptation.

I organized students into groups of four. Each student would have materials to blow his or her own bubbles, but they were to collect the data as a group. Before starting, I asked for a student volunteer to demonstrate how to blow bubbles on a desk. I wrote the steps on chart paper posted on the wall:

1. Place a small puddle of bubble mix on your desk.

2. Place a straw into the puddle.

3. Blow slowly into the straw.

4. Stop when the bubble is the size you want and pop it, or stop when the bubble pops by itself.

5. Measure across the circle to get the diameter and the radius and record on your group's table. The diameter will be where the line across the circle is the widest.

6. Use string to wrap around the circle and find the circumference and record on your group's table.

7. Wipe the desk off and go back to Step 1, trying to create a different-sized bubble.

Andre demonstrated bubble blowing for the class; he poured about a teaspoon of bubble mix onto his desk, poked a straw into the puddle, and blew. A bubble emerged and then popped. The circle left by the bubble turned out to be 5 inches across, so I wrote 5″ in the chart on the board under Diameter. Students knew that the radius would be half that and said the radius would be 2.5 inches. "What about the circumference?" I asked. Markita suggested they wrap a piece of string around the circle and then measure the length of the string.

I explained that with blowing bubbles, they would have to measure quickly, because the bubble outlines would not last long. I encouraged them to start small, blowing circles that were around 2 to 4 inches in diameter. I again reminded students that the tools they were using should be used for the intended purposes *only*. I gave each group a tray that had a plastic cup half full of water, a bubble jar, four straws, several paper towels, and four pieces of string. I allowed five minutes for them to practice blowing bubbles on their desks. (This free exploration was important as it helped them focus on the measuring that followed.) They were very excited about the bubbles they were making and showing each other their various sizes. I then asked students to stop blowing bubbles and to wipe off their desks. I explained that each group needed to develop a table like the one on the board and record the data from each person in the group. "To start, I want you to make smaller circles. Record your information and look for patterns in your data," I explained to the class.

When I saw that each group had its table ready, I asked the students to review what they needed to do. Students responded that they needed to measure right after they popped the bubble, record their measurements, make lots of different-sized circles, and start with small bubbles.

Observing the Students

As I circulated, I noticed students were highly intrigued by what they were finding.

"Look at this! The diameter is one-half inch, the radius is one-fourth inch, and the circumference is three inches," Marcus said to Antonio about his first circle.

In another group, Lydia stretched out her string after she had found the circumference and announced, "Hey, look at my circumference, it's from there to there—eight inches!"

Students also talked to each other about how to measure accurately. "How are you measuring circumference?" Rebecca asked Lindsey.

Lindsey explained, "Start at the end of the string and go around and mark the place where it ends."

In each group, each student was creating bubbles, measuring, and recording his or her data on the group table. One group forgot to find the circumference for their first circles and had to delete some of their data.

After about ten minutes, I said, "Now you can try to make large circles."

One group decided to try having two students blow into the same bubble to see if that would make it larger. Students were highly motivated to find the biggest bubble, but they were still measuring and recording each circle they made. Alex loudly stated, "Hey, I have a circle that I used almost the entire string to measure the circumference!" Similarly, other students were motivated to find small circles. Alyssa reported that she found a circle that had a circumference of $\frac{1}{4}$ inch.

Continuing the Investigation

After another ten minutes, I asked students to put their supplies away and clean off their desks (actually, they were very clean, having had soapy water wiped on them repeatedly!). One student from each group returned the group's tray to a table in the back of the room. The others used the paper towels to make sure their desks were dry.

I explained to students that each group now needed to study its data. I said, "I want you to analyze it as mathematicians. Are there any patterns? Does any of your data look like it doesn't belong? What could have happened in your measuring that might have affected accuracy?"

"With the string, it's hard to see exactly where your finger was on the string," Rebecca explained.

"When you are measuring, it's hard to see where the exact center is," Lucas added.

Markita chimed in, "Once the bubble is gone, it's hard to see exactly where the circle is—the liquid starts to run and you don't know if you are on the exact outline of the circle."

"Keep that in mind as you look at your data. You might see small errors, which is OK, but keep your eyes open for data that doesn't fit and consider why you think that happened. I am going to give you five minutes to look at your data. Then be ready to share any patterns you notice, errors you found, and what you think caused those errors," I directed.

Observing the Students

As students worked, I roamed around and observed the discussions. One group discussed the diameter-to-circumference relationship. Andre had already written ×2 or ×4 or ×3 next to each number in the Circumference column, estimating about how many times bigger than the diameter each one was.

"It looks like it's about four," Andre hypothesized, as he pointed at a few rows where he had recorded ×4.

Alyssa wasn't quite sure and said, "Yeah, but others are times three or times two."

"I think it might be pi," Jason suggested.

After a brief pause, Andre responded, "If you look at all of these, it does look like three is about average." At that, they began using their calculators to find more exact ratios between diameter and circumference.

Another group was not familiar with pi but had more accurate measures than the previous group. They figured out that the circumference nearly always turned out to be a little more than three times the diameter. To push their thinking, I asked the group if they thought their rule would work even for large circles. "Think of a hula hoop," I said. They weren't sure. We had a hula hoop in class and measured a longer string that went across the diameter three times. Together, we held the string around the hula hoop and found that it didn't quite make it all the way around.

Ariella said, "That is what happened in our table—three diameters isn't quite enough to equal the circumference."

Another group discussed the patterns:

"Circumference is diameter times two," Randy noted.

"Where did the two come from?" Micaylah asked.

Randy responded, "I tested it a couple of times and it works."

Madison jumped in, "I remember doing this last year."

Micaylah still wasn't convinced and said, "Two doesn't seem right." A teammate pointed at two specific rows in the table where the circumference was approximately twice the diameter. Micaylah responded by pointing at other columns that were "times three" and "times four." The group continued to search for the most accurate multiple.

Alyssa added two more columns to her table. I asked her why she did that. She said, "I added a column titled 'C divided by D' because

I wanted to find the relationship between these so I wouldn't always have to measure both of these." Her other column was titled $C \div R$. Again, she reasoned that this would help her find a pattern. All the other groups had settled on "about three" as the relationship from diameter to circumference. Wanting them to be more specific, I asked Alyssa to share her strategy with the class. She did, and other groups began using division as a strategy to find a more exact relationship between diameter and circumference and radius and circumference.

A Class Discussion

After another five minutes, I added the new columns to the class table and asked each group to give data for one of its circles. I asked the students to give me a variety of circle sizes. This is the data we collected:

Circle Number	Diameter	Radius	Circumference	$C \div D$	$C \div R$
1	3.5	1.5	10	2.9	6.7
2	5	2.5	15.7	3.14	6.28
3	7.5	3.75	19	2.53	5.07
4	3	1.5	9	3	6
5	6	3	20.3	3.4	6.8
6	17	8.5	50	2.94	5.88

After recording this data, I asked the students what patterns they noticed. Randy stated that the radius is always half the diameter.

"The first circle in the table doesn't fit the rule," Rebecca pointed out.

Andre added, "Yeah, well you can't be exact with the string and ruler, and that's close."

I asked, "How would I figure out the radius if I knew the diameter? How would I find the diameter if I knew the radius?" Students explained that to get diameter you double the radius, and to get the radius, you take half of the diameter. While this relationship seems like an obvious one, this was not the case for several of the students.

"What about circumference?" I asked the class.

Madison said, "Multiply diameter by pi."

Only a few students in the class knew what pi was, so I responded, "Assume I don't know what pi is—can you tell me the relationship you found in your data?"

In this question we had to use bubble stuff to blow bubbles on our desks. When the bubbles popped the made circles. We all measured our circles. We used string to measure the diameter and the circumference. This is the measurements we got.

Circle #	Diameter	radius	Circumference
1	$\frac{7}{8}$	$\frac{7}{16}$	$2\frac{3}{4}$
2	$1\frac{1}{2}$	$5\frac{3}{4}$	$36\frac{5}{8}$
3	3	$1\frac{1}{2}$	$9\frac{1}{8}$
4	$2\frac{1}{4}$	$1\frac{1}{8}$	7

When I looked at the table one thing that I noticed is that when you take and divide the circumference by the diamater like this - (7 ÷ 2.25)= 3.1111 - you get a number that is about 3 every time. This means that the circumference is about 3 times bigger than a circles diameter.
Also, the radius is half the size as the diameter. Because it takes 2 radiuses to equal a diameter and 3 diameters to make a radius, if you divide a circumference by a radius like this - (2.75 ÷ .44)=6.25 - you get a number that is about 6. This is because 3×2 equals 6.
So if you have a string as long as a circumference you can cut it to be 3 pieces as long as a diameter or 6 as long as a radius.

Madison explained, "Well it's about three times the diameter." I asked her where she was getting that information. She said she was looking at the C ÷ D column. Then she added, pointing at the class chart, that some results were more than 3 and some were less than 3, but they should all be 3.14.

Since a student had mentioned pi, and had said it was 3.14, I decided to discuss this approximation of pi. I asked, "What does the 'point fourteen' in pi mean? Is it a lot?" Ariella said that it was like fourteen out of one hundred, which isn't much, so it fit with being slightly more than three.

I then had students choose from a collection of circular objects. I directed them to measure the diameter and multiply it by 3.14 to find the circumference. After multiplying, they used a new piece of string to measure the circumference and see how the two measurements compared.

To close the lesson, I asked them how to use one of a circle's measurements to find the other two. For example, I asked, "If I only have enough string to find the radius, how can I determine the diameter? The circumference?" Then, for their written assignment, I asked them to describe all the relationships they had figured out, for example:

- circumference to diameter

- diameter to circumference

- radius to diameter

- diameter to radius

- pi to diameter

All students were able to accurately describe the relationships among radius, diameter, and circumference. (See Figure 1–1 on page 9 for one student's explanation.)

Earthshine

In the first chapter of the novel *Earthshine*, written by Theresa Nelson (1994), Isaiah tells Slim about the Hungry Valley, a magic valley where the miracle man, the Water of Life, and other miracles can be found. He tells her about the Dragon Trees and the sap of the Dragon Trees, which is called Dragon Blood.

This lesson focuses on the Dragon Blood. A small bottle of this Dragon Blood can be purchased for $50. This Dragon Blood, when rubbed on the skin, is supposed to give the recipient strength and bravery. In this activity, students make standard measurement conversions for bottles of various products to find the price per gallon for each item.

MATERIALS

1 pint-size bottle filled with water colored with red food coloring, to represent Dragon Blood

12 product bottles of various sizes (such as mouth wash, perfume, cough syrup, nail polish remover, and spring water), with the price labeled on each bottle

***Earthshine* record sheet,** 1 per student (see Blackline Masters)

Introducing the Investigation

I began the lesson by reading aloud the first chapter of the novel *Earthshine*, which is four pages in length. In this chapter, we are told that a small bottle of Dragon Blood can be purchased for $50. To launch the lesson, I then told the students that I went to get some Dragon Blood. I showed them a pint-sized water bottle that was filled with a red liquid (red food coloring in water) and explained that it was a $50 bottle. I asked them if this was a small bottle. Some said yes, if you compared it with a liter or a gallon; others said that it was big compared with other bottles they had seen around their house. Most pictured a larger bottle of blood for $50 because $50 a bottle sounded like a lot; others pictured a much smaller bottle. I continued with my story, telling them that it was a long way to the place where I got the Dragon Blood so I wouldn't be able to make frequent trips. I also told them that my friends and family might want some of the Dragon Blood too, so I would probably want to bring back more than 1 pint.

"If I decided to bring back a gallon of Dragon Blood, how much would it cost me?" I asked. "What information would we need to solve this problem?"

Sally answered, "We would need to know how many pints in a gallon and stuff like that." The other students agreed and I reviewed the standard measurement conversions for volume and had them copy them into their notebooks.

1 cup = 8 fluid ounces
2 cups = 1 pint
2 pints = 1 quart
4 quarts = 1 gallon

"How can we use this information?" I asked.

Ben explained, "There are four quarts in a gallon and two pints in each quart, so there are eight pints in a gallon."

I asked, "How is this helpful to us?"

Julie responded, "We know we need eight of those bottles to make a gallon, so we could multiply eight by fifty dollars." Others nodded their heads in agreement.

I then placed on the chalkboard tray the bottles I had brought from home, each labeled with a price. I asked, "What if I wanted to buy a gallon of each of these items? In a moment, you'll figure out how much a gallon of each would cost, but first you'll do some estimating." I distributed a worksheet to each student (see Blackline Masters). (**Note:** The chart on page 13 lists the actual bottles we used in the lesson and that I had recorded on the worksheet. Before duplicating the chart for your class, fill in the names of the bottles you collected.)

I held up the bottles on the tray, one by one. For each, I identified its name, told the students the price on its label, and had them record the price on their worksheets. I told them not to worry about a sales tax. I also told them, "You can write the exact price, or you may want to round it up or down to a friendlier number."

Because I wanted them to do some estimating first, I purposely didn't reveal the amount of liquid each bottle held. After the students had recorded the costs, I told them they would be writing the numbers

Prediction	Item	Amount	Cost	Cost/Gallon
	Dragon Blood			
	Scope			
	V8 Splash			
	Club Soda			
	Balsamic Vinegar			
	Deja Blue			
	Vanilla			
	Worcestershire Sauce			
	Stress Liquid			
	Nyquil			
	Tabasco			
	Cologne			
	Crème de Menthe			

from 1 to 13 in the first column, titled "Prediction." I explained, "At this time, you don't know the actual sizes of the bottles, but I'd like you to think about how much a gallon of each product might cost. Write a one next to the item that you think will cost the most for one gallon, a two next to the item that you think will be the next most expensive gallon, and so on until you've ranked all thirteen items. Talk with the others at your table about your predictions."

The room became noisy with conversation. After a few minutes, I gave a one-minute warning for them to finish their predictions. As the students were finishing, I copied the size of one of the bottles from its label on the board: *8 FL oz./236.57 mL.* Then I called the class back to attention.

I pointed to what I had written on the board. "I copied this from one of the bottles' labels," I explained. "Why do you think there are two measurements on this label?"

"Because we have two measurement systems," David replied. "One is the metric system, which uses milliliters. The other system is the one we use here in the United States. We use fluid ounces." We discussed which measurement we should use to figure cost per gallon, and the general agreement was to use the standard U.S. measurement system. I divided the students into partners and they started to work on the problem of determining the cost of a gallon of each item. They began by taking one bottle, determining the cost, recording it, and then returning the bottle and selecting a new one. There were more bottles than partners so this enabled things to continue moving along. It also allowed students to work at their own pace. Some students looked at all the bottles and others just some.

Observing the Students

As I moved around the room, one of the first questions that I entertained was from two girls working with a bottle of cologne. They couldn't find where the volume of the bottle was listed. I had them turn the bottle over and pointed to the label on the bottom of the bottle. It said 0.5 oz.

"What does it say?" I asked.

"Zero point five ounce," Julie answered.

"What does that mean?" I asked.

"Five-tenths," Sally replied.

"What is that the same as?" I continued.

"One-half ounce," Sally responded after a slight pause.

"Wow, that's small," Julie commented.

"Yeah, it's going to take a lot of these to make a gallon," Sally added.

"What do you need to know to get started?" I asked.

"I think we need to start with ounces in a cup," Sally replied thoughtfully.

"Yeah, and somehow we have to change it to gallons," Julie continued. "I don't know how we can do that."

"I bet you can figure it out. Use the information in your notes to get started. When you figure out something new, add that information to your notes because it might be useful on another bottle," I suggested.

"OK," they responded as they started to work.

I turned to another pair and listened to their conversation. They were working with a bottle of mouthwash that held 33 fluid ounces. They had figured out that 1 gallon is 8 pints or 16 cups. Now they were stuck. "We don't know what to do because this says thirty-three fluid ounces," Jim stated.

"What do you know about fluid ounces?" I asked.

"Well," said Greg, looking at his notes, "there are eight fluid ounces in a cup."

"How can you use that to help you work with the thirty-three fluid ounces?"

There was a long moment of silence as the two pondered the question. Jim started to make some marks on his paper and then remarked, "I guess we can divide thirty-three by eight and get four cups with one ounce left over. What do we do with the extra ounce?"

"Since we are estimating the cost, and one ounce is a small amount compared with this big bottle, why don't you just round this bottle to thirty-two ounces? Does that make it easier to work with?"

"Yeah, lots," Jim replied.

I stood back to watch and listen to them work.

"Thirty-two ounces is four cups and we know how many cups are in a gallon," Jim continued.

"But thirty-two ounces is also a quart," Greg said. "I changed all of these—pints, quarts, and gallons—to ounces and thirty-two ounces is a quart.

"And if you look down here," he continued, pointing to his notes, "there are four quarts in a gallon, so we need four of these bottles."

"I think we can do sixteen divided by four to figure out how many bottles we need because there are sixteen cups in a gallon and this bottle has four cups in it," insisted Jim, who seemed very interested in making his idea work.

"But we don't have to do that because this will work," Greg countered.

At this point I stepped in and said, "I see you've found something that works, Greg, and that's great. I wonder if Jim's way will work, too."

Greg said, "We already have a way that works."

"Yes, it looks like you do, but if you have more than one way to do it, you can use your second way to check your first. If Jim's way also works, then you'll have another way to solve this problem and you might want to use his strategy another time. It's important to understand more than one way to do something," I responded.

"OK," Greg conceded.

"What I think we can do is take sixteen cups in a gallon and divide it by four cups in this bottle. That gives us four bottles. It turns out the same as yours," Jim concluded.

"So then we have to multiply four bottles by about three dollars and we get twelve dollars for a gallon of mouthwash," Greg added. They wrote this down on their paper.

I checked back with Julie and Sally. They had determined that they needed sixty-four bottles of cologne to make a gallon.

"How did you determine that you need sixty-four bottles?" I asked.

"Well, there are eight fluid ounces in a cup, so that's sixteen ounces in a pint and thirty-two ounces in a quart. We need half that, so that's sixteen ounces in a quart. There are four quarts in a gallon, so sixteen multiplied by four equals sixty-four of these bottles," Julie explained very methodically.

"You sure did a lot of thinking. I'm wondering why you said you would need half of the thirty-two ounces in a quart," I inquired.

"Because this is half an ounce; remember, it says point five ounces," responded Sally.

"So how many of these do you need to make an ounce?" I asked.

After a minute or two of thinking, Sally seemed to catch on and said, "Oh, we need two of these for every ounce, not half for every ounce. We messed it all up!"

"No, you didn't mess it all up. I think that you can fix it by doing one thing differently," I said.

"We need to multiply by two, not cut it in half," Sally said. At this, they got back to work.

The next pair had completed several items on the list and was currently working on a quart of juice. "This one is easy," Erin said. "Four quarts are in a gallon, so we need four of those to make a gallon." I continued on to the next group.

Donald and Stan were working on the 2-ounce bottle of hot sauce. "I don't think we're doing this right," Donald said as I walked over.

"What have you done so far?" I asked.

He answered, "We have this hot sauce, which is two fluid ounces and costs three dollars. We have eight fluid ounces in a cup. Two cups are in a pint. Two pints are a quart and four quarts are a gallon. We don't know what to do with the two ounces."

"You have good information here. Now what are you going to do with it?" I asked.

"That's what we don't know," he responded.

"OK, how can you use the eight ounces in a cup to help you?" I began.

"Well, there are two ounces in the hot sauce, so we could divide."

"What would you know then?" I asked.

There was a pause before Stan answered, "There are four bottles of hot sauce in eight ounces."

"How else can you think of those eight ounces?" I asked.

"It's a cup," Stan said.

"And we know how many cups are in a pint, " I continued.

"Oh yeah," Donald said.

"We also could find out how many ounces are in a gallon," I suggested. "How could we use that information?"

"We could divide that by two to find out how many bottles of hot sauce make a gallon," Stan said.

"That's easy because it's just half," Donald said.

As the boys went back to work, I moved on to observe another pair.

Kerry and Megan were working with a bottle of Worcestershire sauce. They were trying to find the number of ounces in a gallon. They had made a list, counting by eight (the number of ounces in a cup) because they knew that there were 16 cups in a gallon. Rather than multiply, they made a list of sixteen consecutive multiples of eight to find 128 fluid ounces in a gallon.

"What do you plan to do now?" I asked when they seemed to have stalled for a few moments.

"We are going to divide that by ten because there are ten fluid ounces in a bottle of Worcestershire sauce. Then we will know how many bottles we need," answered Kerry.

"I did it, and I got twelve point eight bottles," added Megan, looking at her calculator.

"Why don't we say thirteen bottles, because you wouldn't buy eight-tenths of a bottle," replied Kerry. They continued on with their discussion and calculations and I moved on to another group.

As class was about to end, I had the students return the bottles to the chalkboard tray. I asked them to look over what they had done today. As a homework assignment, I asked them to write down an explanation for how they determined the cost per gallon for one of the items on the list. I told them, "Tomorrow, we'll share what we found out today and make a complete list we can use to check our predictions."

Figure 2–1: Beth explained how she made her calculations.

How much will each of these items cost per gallon?

Prediction	Item	Amount	Cost	Cost per gallon
1	Dragons Blood	1 pint	50.00	$400.00
10	Scope	33 fl oz / qt	$3	$12
11	V8 Splash	32 fl. oz	$3.00	$12.00
13	Club Soda	1 Quart	99¢≈1.00	$4.00
4	Balsamic Vinegar	1 qt	$4	$32
12	Deja Blue	20 fl oz	$0.69	$4.14
9	Vanilla	8 fl. oz	$5	$80.00
3	Worcestershire Sauce	10 fl oz	$7	$91.00
5	Stress Liquid	8 fl oz	3.00	$48.00
6	Nyquil	6 fl. oz	$3.50	$72.50
8	Tabasco	2 fl oz	2.00	128.00
2	Escape cologne	.5 fl oz	10.00	$2360.00
7	Crème De Menthe	1 fl. oz	$1.00	128.00

Explain how you converted **one** of the items above into cost per gallon.

There is 4 quarts in a gallon and in the club soda there was 1 quart. So you take 1 quart and turn it into 4 quarts. There it cost 99¢ ≈ 1.00, so the cost per gallon would be 4.00.

Drangons blood - 1 gallon = 4 quarts = 8 pints $50 x 8 = $400.00

Scope = 1 pint = 2 cup   1 cup = 8 fl oz   8)33 32 4

12.8
WorcesterShire Sauce - 10)128 fl oz in a gallon   13 x 7 = 91

1 pint = 2 cups
1 cup = 8 fluid ounces
1 gallon = 128 fluid ounces

8 16 24 32 40 48 56 64 72 80 88 96 104 112 120 128

Figure 2–2: Timothy explained how he solved the problem.

How much will each of these items cost per gallon?

Prediction	Item	Amount	Cost	Cost per gallon
1	Dragons Blood	1 pint	$50	$900
6	Scope	33 oz	$3.00	12.00
5	V8 Splash	1 quart	$3.00	12.00
13	Club Soda	1 quart	$1.00	64.00
12	Balsamic Vinegar	1 pint	$4.00	$32.00
11	Deja Blue	20 fl oz	$1.00	$7.00
4	Vanilla	8 oz	$5.00	$80
7	Worcestershire Sauce	10 oz	$7.00	$45
10	Stress Liquid		$3.00	$44.00
8	Nyquil		$3.50	$73.50
3	Tabasco		$2.00	$128
2	Escape cologne	.5 fl oz	$10	$2,560
9	Crème De Menthe	1 oz	$1.00	$128

Explain how you converted **one** of the items above into cost per gallon.

I'm doing the dragons blood first I went to my notes and found out that 2 pints are in a quart. 2nd I went back to my Notes and found out that there were 4 quarts in a gollon. 3rd I took 8 quarts times 50 and got $400 dollars for a gallon of dragons blood.

The Next Day

The following day, as the students shared their work, I recorded their information on a chart on the overhead. (See Figures 2–1 and 2–2 for two students' tables.) (**Note:** Before the class sharing, you might need to give the students additional work time to complete the tables.) Many students were surprised by the results. Many had predicted that the Dragon Blood would be most expensive per gallon, but were surprised to find the cologne was more expensive. In addition to working on their estimation skills and strategies, students were able to use measurement conversions in a meaningful way.

Eighteen Flavors

"Eighteen Flavors" is a poem in Shel Silverstein's collection *Where the Sidewalk Ends* (1974). The poem describes all the flavors of an ice-cream cone piled high with eighteen scoops. The poem ends in disappointment when the scoops topple to the ground.

This lesson focuses on developing students' algebraic thinking. Students measure the height of a paper ice-cream cone with one scoop of ice cream, then two scoops, three scoops, four, five, and so on. They try to find a general approach for determining the height of a cone with any number of scoops. Then, using n to represent any number of scoops, students try writing an equation for the height of the cone.

MATERIALS

Eighteen Flavors ice-cream shapes, 1 set of 1 cone and 6 scoops per group (see Blackline Masters)

rulers, 1 per group

measuring tapes, 1 per group

scissors, 1 per group

Introducing the Investigation

When I read aloud Shel Silverstein's poem "Eighteen Flavors," the students in my class listened intently and made "ohh," "ahh," "mmm," and "yuck" sounds as I read the various flavors. I asked them why there was a "sniffle" at the end of the poem.

"Because you can't eat it that way . . . off the ground!" Lori said.

"What do you mean?" I asked.

"Because it was sounding so great and they lost it," Lori answered.

"A waste of money," Patty added.

"Does it surprise you that these eighteen scoops would be on the ground?" I asked.

"No, because that's too many for the cone to hold up," Michael answered.

"Holding up your fingers, show me the largest number of scoops you have had on a cone before," I requested. I looked around the room and then added, "Some of you have had as many as four. How many of you have had your ice cream fall off before?" Hands flew in the air. "A number of you have. So you have had very good ice-cream experience to use to solve this problem today."

I asked my students to think about the following question. I held up a sheet with a cone drawn on it along with circles to represent scoops of ice cream (see Blackline Masters). "If the scoops were as big as the circles on this sheet, how tall do you think eighteen scoops of ice cream on a cone would be? Using a sheet of these cones and scoops, try to answer the following questions: How tall is an ice-cream cone with one scoop of ice cream? How tall is a cone with two scoops? With three scoops? Four scoops? Five? Eighteen? Twenty? Fifty? N scoops?" I stopped and recorded the questions on the board:

How tall is an ice-cream cone with 1 scoop of ice cream?

2 scoops?
3?
4?
5?
18?
20?
50?
n?

"What is *n*?" I then asked.

"It's a variable," John replied.

"Why am I writing a variable to refer to scoops of ice cream?" I questioned.

"You're using the variable because the number of scoops can vary. Each time you go to the ice cream store, it can be different," John responded proudly.

"Maybe sometime I just might try to get eighteen flavors on one cone!" I continued. "Who has a prediction about how tall eighteen scoops might be?"

"About seventy-five centimeters," Allison predicted.

"I think a little more, like ninety," Joyce chimed in.

Before the students began to work, I held up a piece of paper with about a dozen numbers written randomly all over it. I said to the students, "I've experimented with this problem a little bit already and here is what I found out. Can you tell what I discovered?"

"No, you don't know which answer goes with which question because it is all disorganized," Anthony responded.

"What could I do about that?" I questioned.

"Use the lines on the paper and list them better," Rochelle suggested.

"Use rows and columns to make a table," Michael offered.

"Those sound like good ideas that I hope you will consider as you work on the problem."

Observing the Students

I organized the students into groups of three or four. I distributed a set of ice cream shapes and scissors to each group of students. Having to cut out the cones and circles gave the students something to do as they began to talk about solving the problem. In a few moments, students asked for rulers and began measuring the cones and the scoops. They used the paper cutouts to build taller and taller ice-cream cones.

Every group had to decide how it was going to stack its scoops on the cone. All but one group decided to have the scoops overlap because, as Mark explained, "That's how it would really be."

"Wow! That's sure more than seventy-five centimeters!" Allison commented about her earlier prediction for how tall eighteen scoops would be.

"Do we want to build a table or do something else?" Lori asked.

"Do you just want to measure the scoops and look for a pattern to start off with? If we can find the pattern to start off with then maybe we won't have to make the table," Kathy suggested.

The First Group

I circulated as the students worked and listened to their conversations. I overheard Allison say, "To figure out the height of each scoop when they overlap, let's just say we would take however much off of each one. How about half an inch? That would be reasonable."

"So each scoop measures four inches and we take off one-half inch. That makes each scoop three and a half inches," Amy continued as she measured a scoop of ice cream.

"The cone is seven inches," James added.

"One scoop and one cone would be ten and a half inches," Allison replied. Allison, Amy, and James began to write this information down in a table each had created on notebook paper; only Eric did not begin writing.

"Let me see yours," James requested of Amy as he tried to record the data in his table.

"I think we should take off one inch because whole numbers are easier to work with," Eric suggested.

"It won't be as accurate. If you measure it, the space they overlap is about half an inch, and an inch would be too much," Amy explained as she held a ruler up to the overlapped portion of the ice-cream scoops.

Allison directed, "This is supposed to be a group activity, so let's take a vote. Who thinks we should use half of an inch?" Allison, Amy, and James held up a hand. "Good, then it's decided that we'll use one-half of an inch," Allison concluded.

"Whatever," Eric conceded with some dissatisfaction.

"Two scoops and one cone would be fourteen inches . . . seven plus three and a half plus three and a half," Allison said as she thought out loud.

"And three scoops would be seventeen and a half. That's three and a half multiplied by three and then you add on seven," Amy said as everyone in the group except Eric recorded this diligently on his or her paper.

"Eighteen scoops would equal seventy inches. See if that makes sense," Allison insisted as she handed her notebook to Eric, trying to get him more involved.

"Yeah, eighteen times three and a half is sixty-three, and add on the seven-inch cone to get seventy," he responded as he checked her work.

"For twenty, just do the same thing," Amy suggested.

"Or just add on seven more inches for those two more scoops," commented James, who had seemed, until this time, somewhat unsure of what everyone was doing and had continued to ask to see what other members in his group were writing down on their papers. "Then to find fifty scoops on a cone, if twenty scoops is seventy-seven inches, then double that for twenty more scoops, and then find out how much ten scoops is," he continued on with this adding strategy.

"That won't work because the cone is seven inches of that total, and we would be adding in more than one cone," Allison insisted.

"I think we did something wrong," Amy said as she looked over her work.

"Let's go back. Five scoops would be five times three and a half, which is seventeen and a half, plus seven is twenty-four and a half," Allison calculated. She continued, "So fifty times three and a half plus seven should work to find the height of fifty scoops if that works for five."

"Oh, I get it," Eric said. "We use three and one-half each time and multiply by the number of scoops. I don't get how to use the variable though."

This group tried without much success to figure out how to write the equation using the variable. Although the students could find and describe the pattern, they were unable to express it using the variable. However, they were able to work through this in the whole-class discussion that followed.

The Second Group

Lori, Sue, Mark, and Paul began by measuring the cone with one scoop on it and writing down the measurement. They then added another scoop and measured again. They overlapped scoops as the other group did, but they measured in centimeters, not in inches.

"Now we can subtract to find out how much that next scoop was," suggested Lori.

"It would be six centimeters," Sue responded as she measured the cone and scoops.

"When we add them on, all the scoops will be the same, except the top one will have a little more because it is not as squished," Lori noticed. She continued with her idea, "We can use the measurement of the cone and the first scoop together and then add on the extra scoops because each extra scoop would add on six centimeters. So to find eighteen scoops, you have to take six centimeters times seventeen and then add on the twenty-five from the beginning part and it gives us one hundred twenty-seven centimeters."

"So you add all the ice-cream scoops in between except for the top scoop and the cone and you add those on last," Sue repeated, trying to clarify this idea. "So now I don't know how to explain it on paper."

"You want to just finish the measuring and calculating first?" Paul suggested.

"OK," Sue responded and the group went back to work, silently filling in the lists the members had started in their notebooks. After a while, Mark spoke up.

"The pattern is that you add six each time you have a scoop, but if you skip one then you can add on the cone with one scoop on it in the end so you can include that little bit extra. So it would be n minus one times six plus twenty-five," Mark stated, sounding very proud. He had written: $(n - 1) \times 6 + 25$.

"This is kind of confusing," Sue shared.

"Yes, but it will get worse as you move on using equations unless you try to figure it out now," Lori said. She went over their reasoning again to help Sue really understand the equation.

The Third Group

Like the other groups, this group of three students started by placing the scoops on their desks and deciding how much each scoop was to be overlapped by the next and deciding how to measure the cone and the scoops.

"Well, this seems fairly simple," Andy started. "If you know what one scoop is, how do you figure out how much eighteen scoops is?"

"Multiply," Joy responded.

"How are we going to find the height of the scoops?" Brad asked.

"We can measure the diameter of a scoop," Andy responded.

"Yeah, and then after we multiply the diameter by the number of scoops, we could add on the height of the cone," added Joy.

Each of them went to work independently drawing a table, measuring, and recording his or her numbers in the table. Every once in a while, Brad looked up from what he was doing to look at the others' tables.

"Maybe it would be easier to take the overlap off first," Andy suggested.

"What do you mean?" Joy asked.

"Well," Andy went on to explain, "to find the height of three scoops of ice cream on a cone, I was doing three times four inches, the height of the scoops, minus three times one-half, the size of the overlap for each scoop. It seems like it would be easier to take four minus one-half and get three and one-half and then multiply that by the number of scoops so you don't have to subtract it later."

"That's what I was doing already," Joy said. "Then you just have to add the height of the cone to the scoops."

"Oh," Andy said as he began erasing his notebook page. Brad also began erasing his notebook page. They continued working quietly, occasionally checking numbers with each other. Finally, Brad asked, "I don't get what to do with n. What number is it?"

"Well, it could be any number," explained Andy to a very confused-looking Brad. "It is a variable and we use it to help explain the pattern that we are using to find the height of the different ice-cream cones. Ours would be three and a half times n plus seven because every time we did the number of scoops, that is n, times three and one-half and then added on the cone, seven." Brad went back to work, writing this in his notebook.

A Follow-up Problem

Two groups finished their ice-cream cone problem fairly quickly and had time remaining. I gave them a bonus problem: *If the cone costs fifty cents and each scoop costs twenty-five cents, how much would one scoop of ice cream on a cone cost? How much would two scoops of ice cream on a cone cost? Three scoops? Five? Eighteen? How about* n *scoops?"* This was a good extension of the problem that

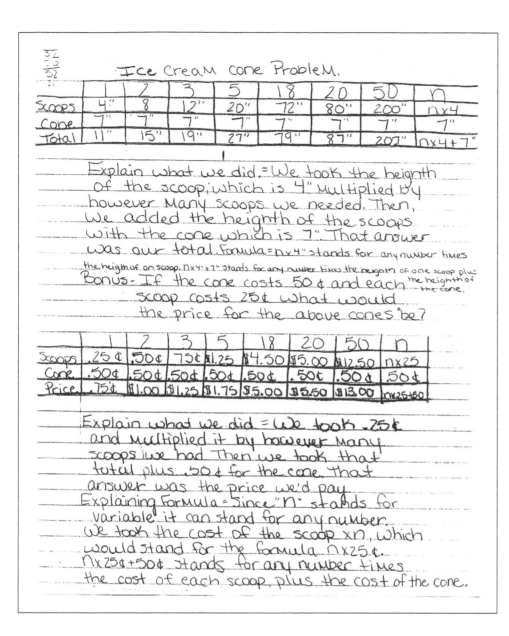

Figure 3–1: Donna's group finished the ice-cream cone problem and then investigated the extension question, which involved the cost of the scoops and cone rather than the height.

required using tables, looking for patterns, and writing an equation. (See Figure 3–1.)

A Class Discussion

In the end, almost every student had a solid understanding of how to find the height of an ice-cream cone with any number of scoops piled on top. Many struggled, however, with writing an equation with a variable. After allowing the groups time to discover the pattern and discuss possible equations, we shared as a class what we had found. This allowed members of the class that had not yet been able to come to a conclusion about the equation a chance to hear what others had done.

Paul began, "We multiplied the number of scoops by three and a half."

"What about for *n* scoops?" I asked the class.

"The same thing you did to all the others, multiply by three and a half," Allison responded.

"But there is no number here to multiply by three and a half, so what should I do?" I asked.

"N could be any number, so you just write down to multiply it by three and a half. Instead of having two times three and a half, and getting an answer, you would have *n* times three and a half and it would just stay that way," Steve replied.

"How were you figuring out your total then?" I inquired further.

"By multiplying the number of scoops by three and a half and then adding on seven for the cone," Andy instructed. "So the equation will end up being the number of scoops times three and a half plus seven."

"The variable means I can change the number of scoops but still do the same thing to find out how tall the ice-cream cone and scoops are. In real life, ice-cream scoops will be different sizes. We could

Figure 3–2: Alan's group considered the "squishing" of the scoops on the cone. The students subtracted a half inch from the top and bottom of each scoop to account for the overlap of the scoops when stacked on top of one another.

	1	2	3	5	18	20	50	n	cone – 7 in.
scoops	3	6	9	15	54	60	150	n×3	scoop – x 3
cones	7	7	7	7	7	7	7	7	overlap
total	10	13	16	22	61	67	157	n×3+7	

They are 3 in because the smash each other
The pattern is take the number by 3
and you get your scoops. The cones
were 7 in. When I got the scoops
I took 7 + the number of scoops
I got and that was my answer.
Ex. 150 + 7 = 157
50 scoops + cone.

I did this because the cones
were 7 in. + the scoops were 3

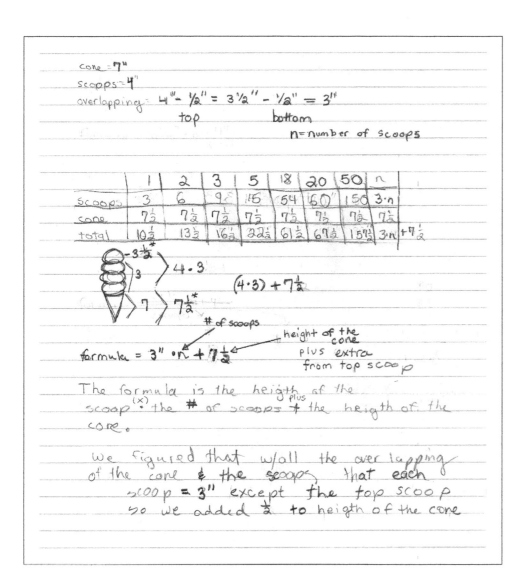

cone = 7"

scoops = 4"

overlapping = 4" - ½" = 3 ½" - ½" = 3"

       top   bottom

                       n = number of scoops

	1	2	3	5	18	20	50	n
scoops	3	6	9	15	54	60	150	3·n
cone	7½	7½	7½	7½	7½	7½	7½	7½
total	10½	13½	16½	22½	61½	67½	157½	3·n + 7½

$(4 \cdot 3) + 7\frac{1}{2}$

formula = 3" · n + 7½

   # of scoops   height of the cone plus extra from top scoop

The formula is the height of the scoop (x) the # of scoops + the height of the core.

We figured that w/all the overlapping of the cone & the scoops, that each scoop = 3" except the top scoop so we added ½ to height of the cone

Figure 3–3: Upon realizing that the top scoop would only be squished on the bottom, Ron added an extra half inch to account for this in the height of the cone for the equation he came up with.

make an equation for today's scoops because we made them so that they are all the same size," I further explained.

We went on to discuss other strategies that students used and other equations that they discovered. After this discussion, I gave the students time to write in their notebooks about their solution strategies and equations and to complete their tables or lists if they hadn't already. (See Figures 3–2 and 3–3.) Students grew in their ability to generalize patterns and record them symbolically.

The Greedy Triangle

The Greedy Triangle, the main character in Marilyn Burns's (1994) story of the same name, is tired of having just three sides and goes to the shapeshifter to get one more side. When he tires of being a quadrilateral, he asks the shapeshifter for yet another side. This continues until he has so many sides, he starts to resemble a circle; at this point he decides to shift back to being a triangle.

This lesson focuses on developing students' algebraic thinking. Students figure out the formula for finding the total degrees of the angles in any size polygon. As a way of determining the total degrees, students first figure how many triangles can be formed when diagonals are drawn from one vertex of a polygon to all the nonadjacent vertices. For example, in a hexagon, it is possible to draw three diagonals from a given vertex, splitting the hexagon into four triangles; therefore, a hexagon has four times as many degrees as a triangle. Regardless of the number of sides of the polygon, there are always two fewer triangles possible, leading to the formula for finding the total degrees: $d = 180 (s - 2)$, where d is degrees and s is the number of sides (or number of angles).

MATERIALS

3-by-5-inch index cards, 1 per student

The Greedy Triangle **regular polygon shapes,** 1 set per group, copied on cardstock (see Blackline Masters)

Introducing the Investigation

My class listened intently as I read *The Greedy Triangle* aloud. After reading the book, I explained to the students that the shapeshifter had a secret formula to find the total degrees of the angles in any polygon, just by using information about the triangle.

"What do we know about triangles?" I asked. The students shared many ideas, including that a triangle has 180 degrees. The students had previously investigated the sum of the angles of triangles. It's important for students to know that the sum of the angles of *all* triangles is 180 degrees. If your students have not learned about the sum of the angles of a triangle, it would be beneficial to do the following activity with them before continuing with this lesson.

To help students make sense of this idea, I had given each student a 3-by-5-inch index card on which to draw a triangle. I encouraged them to make their triangle as irregular as they'd like. I drew one as well and modeled for the students how first to color the three corners of the triangle, then to cut out the triangle, and finally to tear off each of the corners. I explained that I didn't use scissors to remove the corners so that I could easily identify on each torn piece which was a corner of the original triangle. Then I marked a point on the chalkboard and placed my three torn-off pieces so that the corners all touched the point and their sides were touching.

This showed that the three corners of my triangle together formed a straight line, of 180 degrees. After tearing and arranging the angles of their own triangles, students were surprised to find out that the angles of each of their triangles formed a straight line, no matter the shape of the original triangle.

"You, too, can possess the power to figure the total degrees of any polygon," I then told the class. "To get started working on the secret formula, your first challenge is to see if you can find ways that a triangle relates to a quadrilateral, a pentagon, a hexagon, and so on. Also, I want you to think about what happens to the angles of the Greedy Triangle that causes him to begin to roll as he gets more sides."

I organized the students in groups of three and gave each group a set of polygons that I had copied on cardstock (see Blackline Masters). I instructed students to cut out the polygons and trace them to make their own drawings. I then said, "See how you might use triangles to create each polygon. What might be one way to get started?"

"You could put triangles together to try to make the other shapes," Lydia said.

"You could also draw the shapes and then split them into triangles," Phillip added.

To summarize, I said, "So, you are going to use the polygons you have and explore how they relate to triangles. As you work, you may find it useful to organize what you are finding in a table so that you can look for patterns and see what you can discover about the secret formula."

In every group, students cut out their polygons and began to trace each of them. Because we had done other investigations in which they looked at growing patterns, students had become experienced in creating tables as a way of organizing and analyzing their data.

One group recorded a table with columns for the shape name, the number of sides, and the number of angles. Another group created a similar table but also recorded the degrees for an angle. A third group had five columns with shape name, number of sides, number of angles, degrees in an angle, and total degrees. Everyone was working quickly and excitedly, drawing the different shapes, making tables, and trying to find the relationships that would lead them to the shapeshifter's secret formula.

After several minutes of working, I asked students to share the patterns they had found.

"The number of sides and the number of angles are the same for each shape," Jacob said.

"As you go down the table, the number of sides and angles grows by one," Julianna added.

"We found out that if we tried to build the shape from triangles, the number of triangles we needed went up by one each time when the sides increased by one," Hannah explained.

I recorded their ideas on the board and explained that all of these patterns might be useful in finding the secret formula. I noticed that groups were comparing one polygon with another and not focusing on the triangles. I reminded the groups that they were trying to find the shapeshifter's secret formula, which was based on his knowledge of triangles. I asked them to continue exploring and see how they could use triangles to build the other shapes.

One group asked for pattern blocks and began using triangles to make the other shapes. They put two triangles next to each other and formed a parallelogram. They recorded a 2 in the table in a column they had labeled *Number of Triangles*. However, students could not create a pentagon and the hexagon they created used six triangles. The students abandoned the blocks, deciding they weren't helping to find a pattern.

Several groups used their drawings of polygons and began drawing numerous diagonals to find triangles. I interrupted the class to bring everyone's attention to this strategy.

"Several groups are drawing triangles inside the shapes. Can someone share how you are drawing the triangles?" I asked.

Phillip volunteered and came to the board and drew the following:

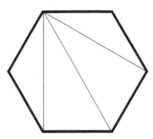

"We just used one vertex and made triangles. You see, with a hexagon, you get four triangles," he said.

"There are more ways," Hannah softly added.

I invited her to the board and she drew the following:

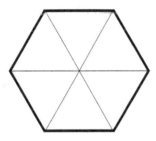

"I have another way," Braden said excitedly. He came to the board and drew a hexagon with even more triangles inside:

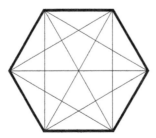

"So we have three drawings. Which can help us find out how many triangles it takes to make a hexagon *and* how many degrees are in a hexagon?" I asked. There was much debate over which drawing would work. Several students argued that the last one wouldn't work because the triangles were overlapping, so you couldn't figure out the degrees. Molly said that the middle one wouldn't work because the angles in the middle wouldn't count in figuring the angles of the hexagon.

I suggested that students go back to their groups and see which of these methods would help them find the degrees in a hexagon the most efficiently.

Observing the Students

I moved around to each group to see what the students were finding. One group believed that it was onto something. Jose explained to me, "You are increasing the area by one hundred eighty degrees each time." I asked him what he meant by "area."

"It's not the area, it's the degrees if you add them up," Isabelle clarified.

"Here, let me show you," Courtney jumped in.

Courtney then drew a picture to demonstrate her group's point. She first drew a triangle and explained that each triangle has 180 degrees. She then sketched a second triangle that shared one side with the one she had already drawn.

"If I put two together, I get four sides. The angles from the new triangle add one hundred eighty degrees to the first triangle."

I encouraged them to keep working and went to another group. Jared explained what they had found. "With more sides, the angles are growing, becoming more obtuse."

"Good observation," I responded. "Keep looking for more relationships like that."

A third group was discussing how many triangles would make a hexagon.

"A hexagon has four triangles," Julianna said.

"No, it has six," Emily argued.

"No, four," Julianna contended, "because with a square you draw a line from one vertex to another. So, the square only has two triangles because—look." She prompted Emily to look at her drawings. (See Figure 4–1.) "One vertex to the other, you can't have overlaps," she explained.

"But with a hexagon, you can make a lot more lines," Emily reasoned.

"But you still can't have overlaps," Julianna explained, pointing at Emily's drawing of the hexagon, which had six triangles in it, like Hannah's drawing on the board.

Emily studied her drawing and saw that the way she had drawn her lines wouldn't work, so she erased them.

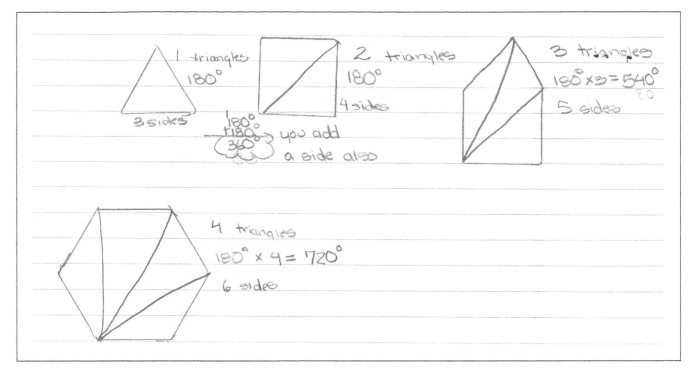

Figure 4–1: Julianna drew diagonals to show how many triangles were needed to create other polygons.

A Class Discussion

After about ten minutes of drawing triangles in the polygons, I called the class together for some whole-group sharing. Lydia said, "I know the secret formula."

"What is the relationship between the number of triangles and the number of sides in the shape?" I asked.

Lydia had created a table that showed how many triangles and how many sides each shape had. (See Figure 4–2 on page 34.)

"Well," she began, "all the polygons with an even number of sides have half as many triangles, wait no." Lydia paused and began to reexamine her table. She noticed that this was true for the quadrilateral, but none of the other shapes.

Michael asked to go up to the board to show how he figured it out. "As the number of sides increases, so does the number of angles, and therefore, the number of triangles, and *therefore*, the number of degrees. Say you're finding how many triangles are in a hexagon." Michael drew a hexagon on the board. "But you have to find how many triangles are in there by drawing a line from one of the vertices to another without overlapping, like Phillip's picture."

Michael turned to the class and asked, "Does everyone agree that a triangle equals one hundred eighty degrees?" The students nodded. "What angles do we measure to get the sum of the angles in

No. A	No. Sides	
1	3	When adding another side you are adding
2	4	another triangle
3	5	
4	6	The Shape setter knew that the number
5	7	of triangles to the number of sides made
6	8	a difference of 2. So he knew that when
7	9	adding a angle/side, there would be
8	10	another triangle.

a hexagon? Not the ones in the very center of the shape where the lines would overlap, right?" The students agreed. "No, you measure the angles where the outside lines of the shape meet. So, you would have to draw it like Phillip has drawn up here on the board with the lines not overlapping, right? Now, does that help you understand how the angles are increasing?" The others seemed convinced.

Observing the Students

Several groups had data collected in tables but weren't sure how to use it derive a formula. (See Figure 4–3.) They returned to working in their groups to try to generate the secret formula. I reminded students that they were to figure out the rule for dividing a polygon into triangles and using the number of triangles to find the total degrees in the polygon.

One group was stumped. I asked questions to help the students find the pattern:

"How many degrees in one triangle?"

"One hundred eighty," Jose answered.

"How many triangles in a quadrilateral?" I asked.

"Two," Jose answered. "That's three hundred sixty degrees."

"That's two times one hundred eighty," Molly added.

"Right, so I need you to look at the relationship between the number of triangles you can draw and the number of sides of the shape. Can you come up with a rule?"

I moved to another group and asked, "What have we found here?"

Lauren answered, "Sides are the triangles plus two."

"And the triangles are the sides minus two," said Jacob. "That could be s minus two."

"So, you've got sides minus two, which happens every time. What about the total degrees of interior angles?" I probed.

"Well, it increases by one hundred eighty every time," Lauren replied.

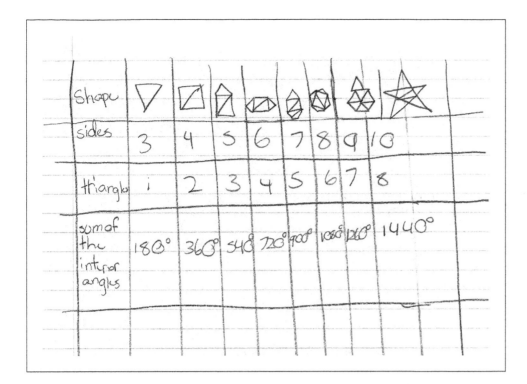

Figure 4–3: Michael created a multiple-row table to show the number of sides, number of triangles, and total degrees of the polygons.

Jacob got excited. He said, "So, the difference is two between the two of them, and the angles are increasing by one hundred eighty degrees every time you add a triangle. So you would have to multiply the one hundred eighty by the number of triangles."

"How would you write a formula so you could plug in any number of sides and know the sum of the angles?" I asked and left them to work on this.

A Follow-up Problem

Each group worked and collaboratively came up with the formula that there are two fewer triangles than the number of sides and that you multiply the number of triangles by 180 to get the total degrees of the angles in the shape. Some groups were able to write it symbolically, while others recorded the pattern in words only. To see whether their secret formula worked, I posed the following problem to the class:

The shapesshifter thinks a 100-sided figure would have a sum of interior angles totaling 17,640 degrees. Use your formula to see if you agree.

With calculators, the groups computed the degrees using their formulas and most agreed.

Molly said, "I don't get it."

Phillip explained. "Well," he said, "if you have the number of sides, you subtract two because that's the number of triangles, then you multiply by one hundred eighty because you add that much every time you add a side."

"I don't agree," Jose said.

"Well," said Phillip, "how many triangles are in a square?"

"Two," Jose replied.

"OK, so you have to subtract two from the number of sides—then how many one eighties are you adding?" Phillip asked.

"Oh, OK, I get it," Jose said.

"Me, too," Molly said.

Emily commented that a one thousand–sided figure would have 179,640 degrees. Students again tried their own formulas and agreed with Emily.

"So, what is happening to each angle?" I asked.

"They are getting bigger," several students stated in unison.

"If a 1000–sided shape is 179,640 degrees, then each angle is 179.64 degrees. That's almost 180 degrees, which would be a straight line!" Elizabeth excitedly explained.

"They are getting more and more obtuse to where they are almost straight," Lauren added.

"Right, so that's how come he started rolling," Jacob began, "but it can never be a perfect circle because it will always have sides, and circles don't have angles."

Figure 4–4: Phillip explained how he discovered the formulas for the number of triangles and angle sum for any polygon. He understood how to generalize the problem, but had just begun to learn to record with variables.

> Next I looked at what the formula was for changing his shape was. I started to look at the number of interior triangles in each shape was The number of interior triangles was increasing by one each shape. Then I also saw that the # of sides was always 2 more than the # of interior triangles. I came up with two formulas. The first was that if S = # of sides and NT = # of interior triangles than the formula: S-2 = NT would work. Then I saw that if a interior triangle was added each time than the angle sum would be increasing by 180. The formula was that if as = angle sum and asns = angle sum of next shape that the formula: as+180 =asns. Than I just found one more S-2 = NT + 180 = as. That is to figure the angle sum. That is what he added in his machine.

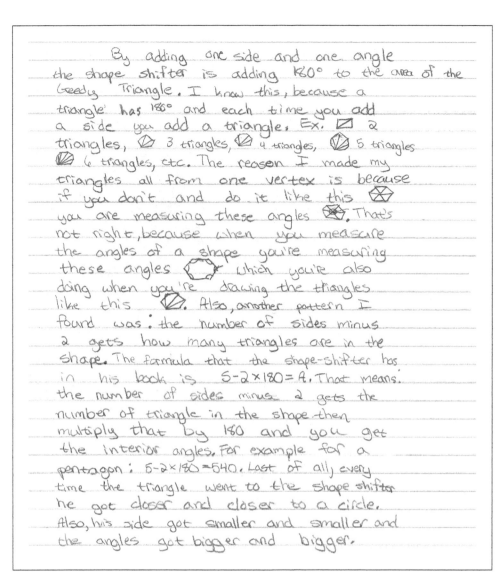

By adding one side and one angle the shape shifter is adding 180° to the area of the Greedy Triangle. I know this, because a triangle has 180° and each time you add a side you add a triangle. Ex. ▢ 2 triangles, ⬠ 3 triangles, ⬡ 4 triangles, ⬡ 5 triangles ⬡ 6 triangles, etc. The reason I made my triangles all from one vertex is because if you don't and do it like this ⬡ you are measuring these angles ⬡. That's not right, because when you measure the angles of a shape you're measuring these angles ⬡ which you're also doing when you're drawing the triangles like this ⬡. Also, another pattern I found was: the number of sides minus 2 gets how many triangles are in the shape. The formula that the shape-shifter has in his book is S-2×180=A. That means: the number of sides minus 2 gets the number of triangle in the shape then multiply that by 180 and you get the interior angles. For example for a pentagon: 5-2×180=540. Last of all, every time the triangle went to the shape shifter he got closer and closer to a circle. Also, his side got smaller and smaller and the angles got bigger and bigger.

Each student prepared a written explanation of how he or she solved the problem. (See Figures 4–4 and 4–5 for two students' explanations.) They worked through this mystery with lots of enthusiasm; in fact, many wanted to keep building new polygons and applying their formulas!

Harry Potter and the Sorcerer's Stone

In J. K. Rowling's *Harry Potter and the Sorcerer's Stone* (1999), the main character, Harry Potter, is a young English boy who discovers he is actually a wizard, not a muggle—a person with no magical ability. One day Hagrid, a very large wizard, brings Harry to Hogwarts School of Witchcraft and Wizardry, the school where all young wizards go. Once there, Harry and his friends encounter many adventures.

Early in the novel, Hagrid is described as twice as tall and five times as wide as a typical person. The description of Hagrid's size prompts this investigation in which students measure their heights and shoulder spans and find the mean, median, and mode of these measurements. They also create a scatterplot to see if there is a relationship between the two measurements. Students can also use the class data and the description of Hagrid's size to create a scale drawing of a middle-schooler and Hagrid. (**Note:** This last activity was not done in the following lesson.)

MATERIALS

yardsticks or meter sticks, at least 1 per group

inch-squared flip-chart paper (or centimeter-squared overhead transparency)

optional: centimeter-squared paper, 1 per student (see Blackline Masters)

Introducing the Investigation

The students listened with delight as I read aloud a portion of Chapter 1 from *Harry Potter and the Sorcerer's Stone*. They were all curious as to how I would tie *this book* into a math lesson.

I stopped reading after I read the passage that describes Hagrid's size. Then I asked, "How big is Hagrid?"

Students repeated the information from the story, that he was twice as tall and five times as wide as a usual person.

I then asked, "How do we find out how tall a 'usual' person is?"

Hands shot up. Elizabeth suggested we find the average height of the students in the class. We had recently worked with measures of central tendency (mean, median, and mode). When I asked what an average was, Lisa said, "We add up the heights of everyone and divide by the number of people."

Arthur said, "It can also be the height that happens the most."

Alonso added, "We could also find the one in the middle."

We decided as a class to measure everyone's height, add up all of the heights, and then divide by the number of students in the class. Then I brought up the issue of measuring accurately. I told them we needed to come up with a consistent way to measure everyone. Anna said that everyone would need to take off his or her shoes before we measured. We decided that was a good idea and that the best way to measure would be to stand up against a wall and use yardsticks or meter sticks.

Then I brought up another issue: units. I asked the students whether they all wanted to use centimeters or inches. There was some disagreement on which to use, but when we put it to a vote, inches won. I created a large table on the chalkboard that had columns for the students' names, their heights, and their shoulder spans (see below).

Name	Height (in Inches)	Shoulder Span (in Inches)

I arranged the students into groups of three. I explained to the students that each group needed to create a similar table for its data and also record its information on my table once the group had finished measuring. I asked them to first measure the height of each person in the group and then we would start over and measure shoulder spans. One member from each group came up and took two yardsticks; each group then found its own area in the room or in the hall where there was a wall that could be used to lean up against for the measuring.

Observing the Students

As the students began to work, I observed many different strategies for measuring. One group decided it would be easiest and most accurate to tape the yardsticks to the wall and just have the person stand in front of them. This proved to be more difficult than the students had planned, for they discovered that one end of each yardstick had an extra quarter inch on it. Melissa said, "Just cover up that last one-fourth inch."

Jessie argued, "You can't do that, it wouldn't be accurate that way!"

Students were concerned about getting accurate measures. As Timothy held the yardstick up to Nathan, he said, "The yardstick is unreliable because it isn't long enough to measure someone."

In another group, students argued about how to hold the yardstick. Sean said, "Hold it straight! Wait, it's not straight, it won't be accurate if it's not straight. You'll be shorter if it's not straight!"

A fourth group had their yardsticks taped to the wall and had each student put his or her back up to the wall to measure. Andrea asked me, "What if it falls in between two inches?" I asked all of the groups to pause and posed the same question to them. As a class, we decided to round to the nearest quarter inch.

Students recorded their heights on the board. As the table filled with measurements, students began to look at the data and notice discrepancies.

Michael said, "Hey, I know I'm taller than Elizabeth, but her number on the board is bigger than mine."

I asked how we should remedy this, and everyone agreed that we should remeasure the heights that were in question. This initial measuring process took longer than expected as students took time to decide how to measure accurately and then had to remeasure in some cases.

The next step was to measure shoulder spans. I told the class that the easiest way would be to have one student stand next to the wall with his or her shoulder touching the wall and have another student measure out from the wall across to the other shoulder with the yardstick. We discussed the importance of having the yardstick perpendicular to the wall, just as the yardstick for measuring height had to be perpendicular to the floor. The second round of measuring went more quickly. Students copied the class data onto their own tables so that they would be easier to analyze and manipulate. Once the data were complete in the class table, several students began to calculate the mean of each measurement (height and shoulder span) with their calculators.

A Class Discussion

I asked the students to stop calculating for a few moments so we could have a discussion. "What is a mode?" I asked.

Amy said, "Um, mode is the most."

I asked, "You mean the number that occurs the most?"

She replied, "Yes."

Then I asked, "What's a median?"

Charlotte said, "The median is the one in the middle." I asked her if she had any special way of remembering that.

She said no, but Michael immediately raised his hand, saying, "I remember it because the median is the middle of the road!"

"Oh, that's a good way to think about it," I replied. Then I asked, "What's a mean?"

Lisa explained, "That's when you add them all up and divide."

Next I asked them how they were going to enter a number like $12\frac{1}{4}$ into their calculators. Nathan said, "One-fourth is point two five on a calculator." I asked him why and he said, "Because twenty-five is one-fourth of hundred."

Next I asked, "Then what is twelve and three-fourths?"

Several students replied in unison that it would be 12.75.

I explained that we were going to find each of these measures of central tendency for our class data about heights. I asked students if they had a good strategy for finding the median. Kendra replied that it would be better if the data were in order from smallest to largest. I said, "OK, so please use a piece of paper to rewrite each person's height in order from smallest to largest."

After students had time to find the class' median height—57.75 inches—I asked, "Is there any way we can check to make sure that the median of fifty-seven point seventy-five inches is accurate?"

Angela said, "We could line everyone up by height." The class agreed this was a good idea, so everyone lined up from shortest to tallest.

I asked, "If there are twenty people in class, where is the middle person?"

Everyone replied, "Ten!" So, we counted in ten from one side and ten from the other, which left two students, Alex and Michael, in the middle. I asked each what his height was. Alex was 57.5 inches and Michael was 58 inches. I asked if that information agreed with the results we had gotten for the median. Elizabeth said, "Yes, because fifty-seven point seventy-five is between fifty-seven and a half and fifty-eight. So the median is right between them."

Alex chimed in with, "Yeah, because twenty-five down from seventy-five is fifty."

Students worked in their groups to find the mean, median, and mode for the shoulder span data, just as they had done for the height data.

To conclude this part of the investigation, I asked students to think back to the book. Hagrid was fives times as wide and twice as tall as a typical person. Could we now figure out about how big Hagrid was? We discussed which of the measures to use—mode, mean, or median. Students decided that either the median or the mean would be good choices because they more accurately represented the middle of their data. Using a median of 57.75 and mean of 57.61 for height, and a median of 14.5 and a mean of 14.275 for shoulder span, they figured that Hagrid must be about $9\frac{1}{2}$ feet tall and about 6 feet wide!

A Follow-up Activity

I next asked students, "Do you think there is a relationship between a person's height and a person's shoulder span?" They looked at the class table of data and shared various ideas. Most students thought that a taller person would have a wider shoulder span. Alonso said, "If you divide the mean for the height by the mean for the shoulder span, it's about four times, so maybe the shoulder span is one-fourth of a person's height."

Some mentioned that the relationship wasn't always the same, pointing to some specific names on the chart that didn't fit that rule. Elizabeth said, "Why don't we divide the height by the shoulder span for every person and see if those are the same?" I said this was a good idea, but we were going to look at the data in a new way to help us see if there was a relationship. I posted a piece of inch-squared flip-chart paper on the board. I drew two axes and labeled the horizontal (x) axis *Shoulder Span* and the vertical (y) axis *Height*. As a class we decided how to scale the graph. We decided to count each square on the x-axis as a half inch so the data wouldn't be too crowded. We also decided not to start the scales at zero, but to start at 10 inches for shoulder span and 50 inches for height, so that the

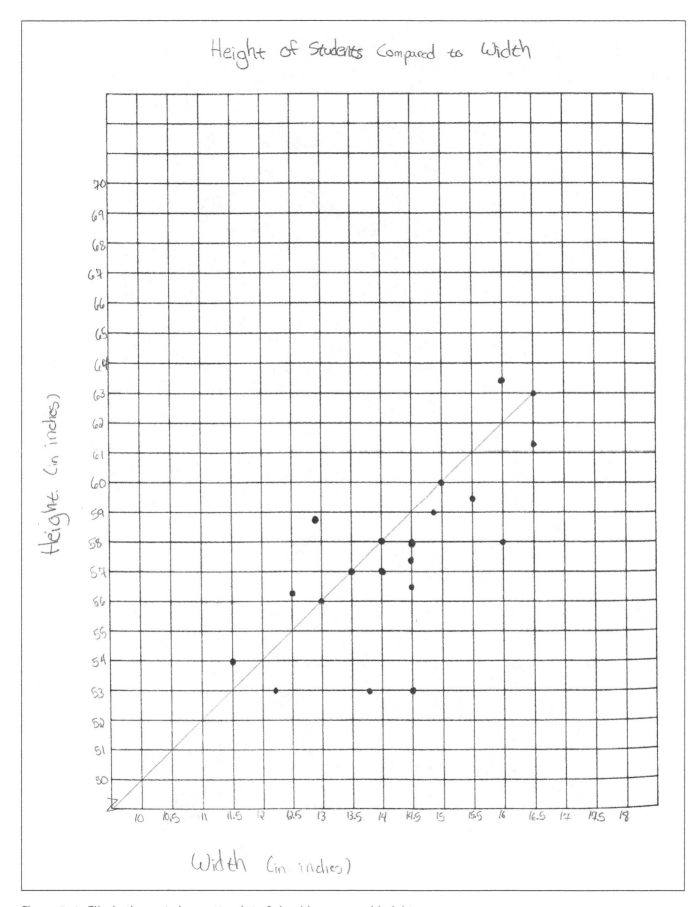

Figure 5–1: Elizabeth created a scatterplot of shoulder span and height.

data would fit on the graph. Each student came up to the chart and plotted a point to represent his or her measurements. As I created the scatterplot on the chart paper, students created their own scatterplots on centimeter-squared paper. (See Elizabeth's scatterplot in Figure 5–1.)

This was the students' first experience with a scatterplot and it prompted excellent discussion about what it means to have a relationship between two variables, in this case height and shoulder span. Nathan said, "The people who were the tallest were also the widest." Others noted that in general, the taller people had the wider shoulder spans. I asked a student to come up and place the yardstick so that it went through the middle of the data points, showing the trend. Markita said, "Maybe some of the points are off because we didn't measure exactly right."

Alex added, "That's true, but even so, each person isn't going to be exactly on the line."

I posed a question to the class: "So, even though many students don't fall on the line, do you think there is a relationship between the two variables?" Students shared various ideas with the class and then I asked them to each write an explanation of their thinking. (See Figures 5–2 through 5–5.)

In conclusion, we tried to plot Hagrid's estimated measurements on the scatterplot. His data was off the chart, but it was clear that

Figure 5–2: Melissa calculated the approximate relationship between width and height.

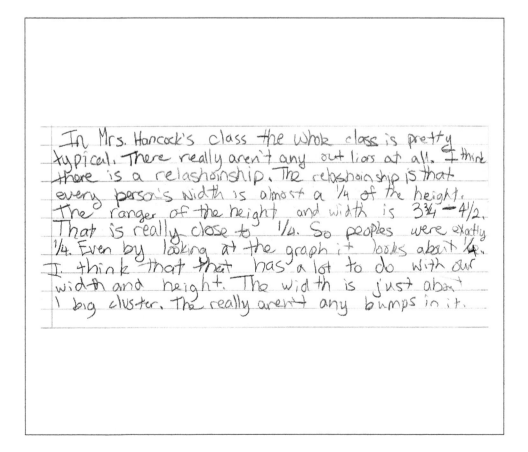

Math and Literature, Grades 6–8

> The similar things between height and width. The people who were the tallest were the widest. It makes sense - tall people are usually wide people.

Figure 5–3: Nathan explained the logical relationship between height and width.

> In this class I think there is a relationship. The people in this class are almost all the same height, 53"–63". They are also almost the same width, 11½"–16½". There really are no outliarers, it's just one big cluster. It is almost all along a diagonal line.

Figure 5–4: Michael used the similarities of class-mates' heights and widths to justify the relationship between the two measurements.

> ### Generalization
>
> The heights that occured the most often were 53" and 58". The number in the middle for height is 57.75". Last of all, the average hight for our class was 57.61". The width that occured most often for width was 14.5", and the middle number for width was also 14.5". The mean for the width was 14.275". Also, when I made the graph I made a diagonal line, and most of the dots were near it, so the data is linear, so there is a relationship. Last of all, I divided each persons height by their width. I got a range of 3.6–4.6 which is only 1 inch away, so that also proves that there is a relationship between a person's hight and width.

Figure 5–5: Elizabeth used statistics from the lesson to explain the relationship.

his data point wouldn't fit along the line we had created. Students reasoned that if *both* his height and shoulder span were twice as big (or five times as wide), then it would be on the line they created. As it is, Hagrid's data point would be significantly below the line, since his width was five times larger and his height was just twice as big. This ninety-minute exploration enabled students to get experience in measuring accurately and in analyzing statistics in order to draw conclusions. Students were highly engaged and reluctant to stop at the end of the investigation.

How Big Is a Foot?

In *How Big Is a Foot?* by Rolf Myller (1962/1990), a king wants to give the queen a birthday present, but the queen already has everything. The king decides to give her a bed; the queen doesn't have one because they haven't been invented yet! The king uses his feet to determine the size of the bed and sends his measurements in king's feet to the apprentice. The apprentice then measures with his own feet and builds the bed, which turns out to be too small. The story concludes with the apprentice figuring out why the bed was too small and resolving the problem.

This activity focuses on proportional reasoning. The apprentice's foot is a fraction of the king's foot. Students determine how many steps the apprentice will need to take to make a bed that is equivalent to six king's feet in length and to three king's feet in width.

MATERIALS

centimeter-squared paper, 2–3 sheets per group available

rulers, 1 per group available

yardsticks, 1 per group available

Cuisenaire rods, 1 set per group

Introducing the Investigation

I began the lesson by showing the class the cover of *How Big Is a Foot?* Students immediately predicted what they thought would happen in the story, with several getting at the idea of standardized and nonstandardized measurement.

I began to read the book to the class. The students chuckled when the king asked the queen to put on her pajamas and lie on the floor so that he could measure around her. It soon became apparent that the problem in this story did in fact stem from the lack of a standardized measurement system.

When I finished reading the story, I asked the students a question: "If the king had not sent over the marble copy of his foot but the apprentice knew that his own foot was half the size of the king's, could he still make the bed? How many apprentice's feet would be needed?"

Sue argued that if the apprentice's feet were half the size of the king's, he would need two of his feet to measure each king's foot. Larry suggested that we draw a picture of a bed and include both the king's feet and the apprentice's feet.

At this point, I asked the students to return to their tables to work in groups of four. I asked them to discuss how the apprentice would measure the bed and then have a group member sketch it on paper.

After the students completed their drawings, I asked, "What other ways could we illustrate the number of apprentice's feet needed to equal the king's feet?"

Joe said, "We could make a table and record the number of feet."

I asked the groups to talk about what this would look like and have a different member of each group write their ideas out on paper.

After giving them several minutes to do this, I prodded for additional ideas. "Any other ways we could represent this relationship?" I asked.

"We could use graph paper to mark the number of feet that would be needed by both of them," Donna suggested.

I asked the students how we should start. Margaret explained, "Since the apprentice's feet are half the king's feet, the king's feet need to be two squares long and the apprentice's feet should be one square long." Using centimeter-squared paper on an overhead transparency, I drew six king's feet, two squares in length for each foot, along the left side of the paper going the length of the paper. Along the inside of the paper, I drew apprentice's feet in each square, showing that an apprentice's foot is half the king's foot. We found that the number of apprentice's feet was double the number of king's feet, just as we expected. (See Figures 6–1 and 6–2.)

"What equation could we use to show this relationship?" I asked.

Figure 6–1: Joan figured that it would take twice as many of the apprentice's feet to equal the same distance as the king's feet; therefore, she multiplied the number of king's feet by two.

1.) 3   6
    ×2   ×2
    6   12
   Width / Length

The apprentice foot is half the size of the kings foot. So the apprentice would have to double his steps to eoqual the kings measurment.

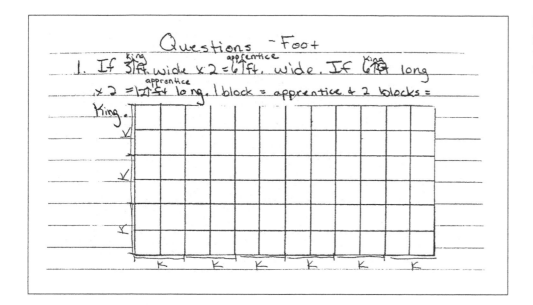

Figure 6–2: Edward used graph paper to illustrate that one king's foot equaled two apprentice's feet.

"We could say that *k* equals two *a*," Jerry answered. I wrote on the board:

$$k = 2a$$

"These are all great representations," I said, "and they may be useful in the next problem, so keep them in mind. In the next problem I would like you to consider in your group how many apprentice's feet would be needed if the apprentice's foot were two-thirds of the king's foot. Discuss this problem with your group. Each person then needs to write his or her answer and explain it."

I wrote the task on an overhead transparency and verbally explained it to the students. The students went to work. Immediately several groups began to discuss how this situation would look in a picture.

Observing the Students

One group drew one king's foot and next to that drew one apprentice's foot that appeared to be about two-thirds of the king's foot. The students didn't seem to be actively working on a plan, and as I approached them, they said, "We don't know what to do next." I looked over what they had done so far and said, "I don't think you've got enough in your diagram yet to see a pattern. Why don't you continue with the idea you have and see if a pattern emerges?"

"It's kind of hard to do it with two-thirds," Andy replied.

"Maybe you should consider approaching the problem another way," I encouraged. "I would be happy to provide you with whatever materials you need."

A few minutes later, one of the students from this group approached me and asked me for masking tape. I directed her to the tape without much thought because I had moved on to another group, and she returned to her group. A few minutes later, she came back and asked for a permanent marker. Now I was curious. I told her where to get a marker and watched her go back to her group, which had now moved to the floor behind their desks. When I finished with the group I was working with, I headed back to the previous group. The kids were busy measuring and cutting pieces of tape 12 inches long, marking each piece with a *k* and placing six of them end-to-end on the floor. These six pieces of tape represented the king's feet.

"We have to figure out how big the apprentice's foot would be now," Larry said to the group.

Janie had a ruler lying in front of her and was marking off 4-inch increments with her fingers. "It would be eight inches," she concluded.

"How did you get that?" Sue asked.

"Twelve divided into thirds is four and you multiply that by two for two-thirds and you get eight," Janie explained.

"OK, I see," Sue replied.

As I walked away, they were measuring and cutting pieces of masking tape 8 inches long, marking each piece with an *a* (for apprentice) and placing the pieces alongside the tape for the king's feet, creating a sort of life-size version of the bed. (See Figure 6–3.)

As I circulated the room, I listened to a group discuss how to proportionally draw the king's foot and the apprentice's foot on graph paper. I observed another group convert the king's foot to 12 inches and the apprentice's foot to 8.

Figure 6–3: Janie's group had difficulty representing the task in a scaled-down version, so it made a life-size model. The kids used masking tape and a ruler to create the outline of a bed on the classroom floor. Janie wrote an explanation of what they did.

> We decided to show you problem # 2. The apprentices foot is 2/3 the size of the Kings. One foot (King) is 12 inches, and 2/3 of 12 inches is 8 inches. We taped a bed that is 6 feet long on the floor. and 3 feet wide. We measured 4 inches against the 6 feet twice to get 2/3. and made a mark. We kept on doing that process until we got to the 6 (Kings) foot mark. We got 9 feet (Appr.) long. Then we did the same process and came up with 4½ (Appr.) feet wide.

"See, this is what I mean," said Don, showing the work he had done on a piece of paper. "If we multiply six king's feet by twelve inches, we get seventy-two inches total. We can divide that by eight inches and we can figure out that we need nine apprentice's feet."

After a brief pause, Melissa added, "And since the width is half the length in king's feet, it would be half the length in apprentice's feet, so that would be four and a half."

One of the students in another group asked me if he could use "those block things that we used when we learned about fractions."

"Do you mean Cuisenaire rods?" I asked.

"Yeah," he replied. I told him he and his group could use any materials they thought could help them solve the problem.

After a short time, the students in this group chose the three-rod to be the king's foot. They picked the two-rod to be the apprentice's foot. They built the bed six king's feet (six three-rods) long and three king's feet wide. Alongside the rods representing the king's feet, they placed the rods representing the apprentice's feet. They then counted the rods to find out how many apprentice's feet would be needed to measure the bed. For the length of the bed, the number of apprentice's feet turned out to be exactly nine; however, for the width of the bed, it was four whole apprentice's feet and part of another. The students discussed how to count the last rod that "hung over" the king's rod. (See Figure 6–4.)

The following day, students revisited their strategies and solutions and shared them with the class. They were very interested in the different representations that their classmates had used to solve this problem. (See Figures 6–5, 6–6, and 6–7.)

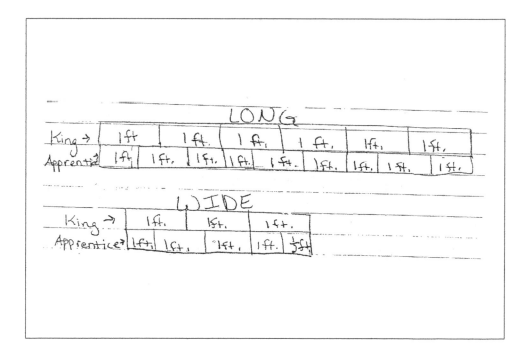

Figure 6–4: Edward's group used Cuisenaire rods as a strategy for working with two-thirds. The students found a rod that equaled three cubes to represent the king's foot. They found a rod that equaled two cubes to represent the apprentice's foot.

Figure 6–5: Stan's group
determined the number of
king's feet in the perimeter
of the bed. The group
members used the reason-
ing that there are three
apprentice's feet for every
two king's feet. They found
the number of groups of
two king's feet and multiplied this by three to find
the perimeter of the bed in
apprentice's feet.

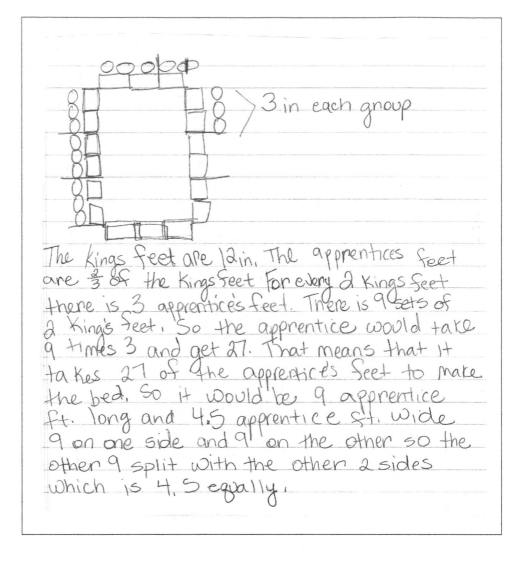

3 in each group

The kings feet are 12in. The apprentices feet are ⅔ of the Kings feet. For every 2 Kings feet there is 3 apprentice's feet. There is 9 sets of 2 King's feet. So the apprentice would take 9 times 3 and get 27. That means that it takes 27 of the apprentice's feet to make the bed. So it would be 9 apprentice ft. long and 4.5 apprentice ft. wide 9 on one side and 9 on the other so the other 9 split with the other 2 sides which is 4.5 equally.

Figure 6–6: Joan's group
used proportional reason-
ing, which is illustrated in
her paper, to determine the
length of the bed.

2.) The apprentice only takes up ⅔ of the kings foot. The apprentice could keep steping foward until he got one of the kings foot which would be 2 ft. He would keep walking until he has taken 9 steps to equal 6 of the king's feet.

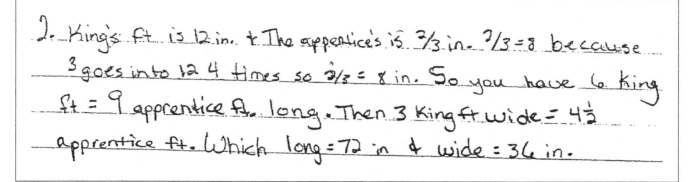

2. King's ft. is 12 in. + The apprentice's is ⅔ in. ⅔ = 8 because 3 goes into 12 4 times so ⅔ = 8 in. So you have 6 King ft = 9 apprentice ft. long. Then 3 King ft wide = 4½ apprentice ft. Which long = 72 in + wide = 36 in.

Figure 6–7: Jerry's group converted the king's foot to 12 inches and used that to find the total number of inches in the length and the total number of inches in the width. The group then divided the total number of inches by 8 because they determined that to be the size of the apprentice's foot.

A Follow-up Problem

"I have one more problem for you to consider today. If we look back at the book, we see that the two beds are not the same size. What kind of measurement are we talking about here?" I asked.

"Length and width," Amber answered.

"The areas of the beds are not the same either," Ryan commented.

I asked the students to look at the two situations we had considered the day before, one in which the apprentice's foot measured half the king's and the other in which the apprentice's foot measured two-thirds of the king's foot. I asked them to determine how the area of the bed would be affected in these two situations if the apprentice had used his own feet instead of the king's feet. I wanted them to see if the change in area was related in some way to the change in length.

Students discussed this new problem in groups. Most groups asked for graph paper and drew diagrams of the beds. After discussing how to draw the king's feet and the apprentice's feet on the paper, they made rectangles on the paper to represent two beds. Each group discovered that if the apprentice's feet were half the size of the king's feet, the area of the apprentice's bed would be one-fourth the area of the king's bed.

I asked my students why this made sense.

"If you just doubled the length, then you would be able to fit one more apprentice bed inside the king's bed. Since you also double the width, then you can fit two more apprentice beds inside the king's bed, making a total of four beds," Sam explained.

Beth added, "It's like you're doubling it and then doubling again. If you had one penny and doubled it you would have two pennies. If you doubled it again you would have four pennies. It all happens because you double the length *and* the width."

Figure 6–8: Teresa drew a grid to illustrate the area of the bed using king's feet compared with the area of the bed using apprentice's feet to determine that the area of the apprentice's bed was one-fourth the area of the king's bed.

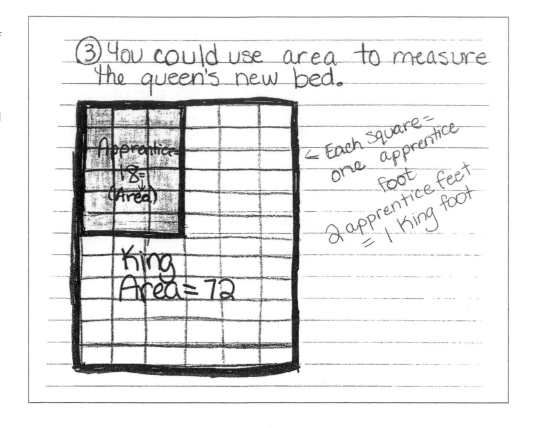

"Yeah, and if you do one-half multiplied by one-half, you get one-fourth. That's how big the apprentice bed is compared with the king's bed," Peyton continued.

Students continued to look at relationships between length and area, drawing pictures and conjecturing about the relationships. (See Figure 6–8 for one student's work for this activity.)

This lesson engaged students in using multiple representations to solve a problem. Groups approached the proportionality in different ways, as the student work illustrates, and applied their proportional reasoning to both length and area measurements.

How Much Is a Million?

David M. Schwartz's picture book *How Much Is a Million?* (1985) provides readers with many illustrations to help them conceptualize large numbers. While million, billion, and trillion are numbers often used in the news and are familiar to students, kids often underestimate how very large these numbers are.

This investigation begins with an introductory estimation activity to encourage students to think about what hundreds of objects look like. Then student groups randomly select different types of measurement (length, area, volume, weight) and develop their own illustrations of how big a million is. To complete this project successfully, students need to measure accurately, complete calculations with measurements, and perform conversions.

MATERIALS

2 different-sized jars (such as 16 ounces and 32 ounces)

2 different-sized scoops (dry-food measuring cups can be used)

2–3 bags of candy corn (or other small objects)

bowls for the candy corn, 1 per group

rulers, 1 per student

transparency of *How Much Is a Million?* instructions (see Blackline Masters)

***How Much Is a Million?* measurement cards,** 1 card per group (see Blackline Masters)

balance or scale

Introducing the Investigation

Before class, I counted how many candy corn filled the larger jar. I left that jar full but left the smaller jar empty. To begin the lesson, I held up the smaller jar and a bag of candy corn. I asked students to record on a piece of paper how many pieces of candy corn they thought would fill the jar and then asked several students to share their estimates.

Next, I asked for a volunteer to come up and fill the small scoop with candy corn and empty it into the jar. Lydia volunteered and emptied one scoop into the jar. I asked her to count how many candy corn fit into the scoop. She took another scoop, counted the pieces, and found that the scoop held eighteen pieces of candy corn.

At this point, I asked the class if anyone wanted to revise his or her estimate. All the students wanted to change their estimates because they realized they had picked numbers that were too small. This time, they used the benchmark of the number of candy corn that fit in a scoop—eighteen—to determine more accurate estimates. Once they had recorded their new estimates, another volunteer, Ricky, came forward and emptied scoops of candy corn into the jar until it was completely full. It held thirteen scoops in total. The students used their calculators to figure out how many pieces of candy corn were in the jar, given that the scoop held about eighteen candies.

I asked the students whether they thought our answer of 234 candies was accurate.

Kendra commented, "There might not always be eighteen candies in the scoop."

"That's true," I responded. "So, can we calculate the number in the jar by multiplying eighteen by thirteen?"

Tyler raised his hand and said, "It would be more accurate if we actually counted every candy."

"I agree," Lisa added.

Michael countered, "That would be more exact, but it would take forever; this way we know about how many are in there a lot quicker."

"The multiplication way will end up being very close to the counting way," Jacob explained, "and we don't really need the exact number to see if our estimates are close, do we?"

The question was directed to me and I redirected it to the class, asking, "What do you think? Is an approximate number of candies good enough to tell if you made a good estimate?"

Several students agreed with the argument that they didn't need an exact count in order to see if they had made close estimates.

I next showed the class the larger jar. I had already filled this jar and knew that 418 candies were in it. Again, I asked students to estimate how many pieces of candy corn were in the jar and record their estimates. This time their first estimates were more reasonable.

Then I showed students a slightly larger scoop and asked them to estimate how many of these size scoops of candy corn would fill the jar. I asked if anyone had a good strategy for making this second estimate. Elisa raised her hand and said, "Couldn't we figure out how many go in one scoop and divide into how many we think are in the jar?" Several students voiced their support of this strategy. Manuel came up, filled a scoop, and counted. It held thirty-one candies. I then shared with them the total candies in the jar and how many scoops it took to fill it.

I then asked, "How big would the jar be if it took one thousand candies to fill it? What about ten thousand candies? One hundred thousand? A million?" I asked them to each discuss the problem with the person sitting next to them. Then, several students shared their ideas with the whole class.

"A jar twice as big as that one would hold one thousand," Korey said, pointing at the bigger jar.

"Then ten thousand would be twice as big as that," Jaylyn added.

Isabelle argued, "Twice as big would only hold two thousand. It would have to be even bigger to hold ten thousand."

"Oh yeah," Jaylyn said after a brief pause. "So, then, it would take five jars that hold twice as many as one thousand."

"How big do you think a jar holding a million would be?" I asked.

"Like a trash can," Mark asserted.

Tyler said, "It would be even bigger than that, like as big as that cabinet." He pointed to a floor-to-ceiling cabinet in the back of the room.

I then introduced the book *How Much Is a Million?* After reading the book, I asked students if they thought their estimates of how big a jar would have to be to hold a million pieces of candy corn were accurate. Some said yes, others no. I placed a transparency on the overhead and explained their next task (see Blackline Masters). Then I organized the students into five groups, with four or five students in each. I gave each group a bowl of candy corn to place in the middle of the table and gave each student a ruler and a calculator. I held out the deck of measurement cards to each group, face-down, and had each group draw one card. If the group picked the weight card, for example, its task was to find out how much a million pieces of candy corn would weigh and then come up with a familiar comparison that would help the class comprehend the measurement. I explained that they needed to measure to the nearest millimeter, gram, or eighth of an inch, depending on the type of measurement they'd be doing.

Observing the Students

As the students worked in their groups, I listened to their conversations and helped as needed. The students working on height were busy thinking about their comparison.

Ladandra said, "Are we going to measure height with the candies end-to-end or side by side?"

"It will be a lot taller if we do it end-to-end," Mark commented.

"Let's do it that way," Jaylyn suggested.

Three of the group members held candies up to their rulers. One student measured with the candy corn leaning against the front of the ruler. Another student had one candy corn standing on the table and had the ruler perpendicular to the table. A third student placed the candy corn on the top of a book and held the ruler next to it. They each got different measures and debated over how to get a good measurement.

"Lisa, your measurement is too small because, look, your ruler has this space before the zero and you can't use that part," Jaylyn said.

Korey said, "Does it matter if the candy corn is leaning? It seems like if it is straight it is not as tall."

"Let's see," Ladandra said, holding the candy corn to the ruler straight up and down and then at a slant. "Well, it's barely different, but that isn't going to make a big difference in our measurements."

I interjected, "What do you all think about what Ladandra said—is it very different? Would it make a difference when looking at one million?"

The group continued to discuss the situation and decided to measure the candy corn straight up. The students placed it on top of a piece of cardboard to account for the space that was at the beginning of the ruler before the zero.

The group finding the weight of 1 million pieces of candy corn began by using the scale. I asked the students what their plan was and Thomas said, "We are going to see how much ten pieces weigh because ten goes into one million easily." They found that ten pieces weighed 15 grams.

Kiera began to do division on her paper to see how many tens were in 1 million. She said, "OK, ten goes into one million a hundred thousand times, so all we need to do is multiply fifteen grams by one hundred thousand." Ally calculated that the total weight was 1,500,000 grams. The students were excited and thought they were done.

I reminded them they had to come up with a visualization that would make sense to everyone to explain what 1,500,000 grams was like. André took out his math book and found the conversions for the metric system and said, "Look, we can change it to kilograms. It takes one thousand grams to be one kilogram."

Ally reached for a calculator, typed in some numbers and said, "OK, then it's fifteen hundred kilograms."

I again asked, "Is that something that the rest of us can visualize?"

"Let's change it to pounds," Kiera suggested. "Everyone knows those better."

André found the conversion in the text and they calculated that the candies would weigh 334 pounds. The group was stuck for a few minutes and then Thomas jumped in, saying, "I know, I know! I weigh one hundred ten pounds, so it is pretty close to three of me."

Reporting the Findings

Once each group had measured its candies, figured the area, length, weight, or volume of one million pieces of candy corn, and found its comparisons, each group had a turn to present its findings. The length group reported that one million candies would stretch about thirteen miles, which was the distance from the town the school was in to a neighboring town. The height group compared one million candies to the height of the Sears Tower, which they had found a picture of on the Internet. The area group looked on the NFL website and found that one million pieces of candy corn would almost cover the end zone of a football field (4800 square feet). The volume group reported that a million candies would fill about three hundred one-gallon milk cartons and they showed how much of the room would be needed to hold that many cartons. Hearing reports of what one million candy corn look like in length, area, and volume was effective in helping students understand the magnitude of one million.

Jim and the Beanstalk

Jim and the Beanstalk, by Raymond Briggs (1970), is a sequel to *Jack and the Beanstalk*. In this book, Jim meets up with the giant, who has grown very old since his meeting with Jack years back. The aging process has caused him to have bad eyes, worn teeth, and a loss of hair. Jim befriends the giant and helps him by getting him bifocals, false teeth, and a wig.

Dealing with the size of these objects is an obvious challenge for Jim and provides the context for applying proportional reasoning to body ratios. This lesson presents students with a specific problem related to the story for which they have to measure, calculate, and reason proportionally.

MATERIALS

loaf of bread
rulers, 1 per group of three students
measuring tapes, at least 1

Introducing the Investigation

To begin the activity, I read *Jim and the Beanstalk* to my students. Then I returned to the part where the giant claims he is going to eat three fried boys on a piece of toast and posed a problem to the students: *How large does a piece of toast need to be for three boys to fit on it?* I explained that I was going to organize them into groups of three and that each group was going to have to come up with the size of a slice of bread that would fit the three of them. To stimulate their thinking, I asked, "What do you need to know in order to solve this problem?"

"We need to know how big the kids are," Alicia replied.

"What do you mean by 'how big'?" I probed.

"We will need to know how tall they are," Alicia clarified.

"And how wide, too," Dan added. "They have to fit both length-wise and widthwise because the bread is like a rectangle."

"OK, so you will need to do some measuring," I confirmed. "With your group of three, figure out the size of a piece of bread that is just large enough to fit the three of you and is the same shape as a typical slice of bread." I had a loaf of bread available so that each group could have a slice as a reference. This would be particularly important for the follow-up questions I planned to pose.

I continued, "After you have figured out and drawn a diagram on paper that includes the dimensions of your slice of bread, I'll give you masking tape to tape the outline of your bread on the floor. Later, each group will try out its piece of toast in front of the class."

Observing the Students

Students used their own dimensions to determine the length and width of the giant's toast. Some groups measured all three members' height with rulers or tape measures before they realized that they needed only the height of the tallest person. Other groups figured this out right away and measured only the tallest person. Students approached finding the width of the slice of bread in different ways. Some students measured each person individually and added these measurements together. Others lay down on the floor side by side, marked the outside edges of their group, and measured that distance. One group found the distance around each of the group members' shoulders with a tape measure. A student from another group challenged them, asking if they were going to roll around on the floor. At first the students who had done the measuring didn't understand what they had done wrong, but after thinking about it for a minute or two, they laughed and took their measurements again, this time measuring across the front of their shoulders only.

When groups finished measuring, drawing, and labeling their rectangles on paper, they asked for the tape. Before giving a group the tape, I talked with them about the shape of their slice of bread. (The loaf of bread I had supplied had slices that were almost square.) I reminded groups that they had to make sure that three people could fit while keeping the shape of the bread similar to the shape of the real bread. Students in each group determined that because their height measurement was bigger than their combined widths, they had to make a square slice of giant's bread by using their height measurement for the length of the sides. (See Figure 8–1.)

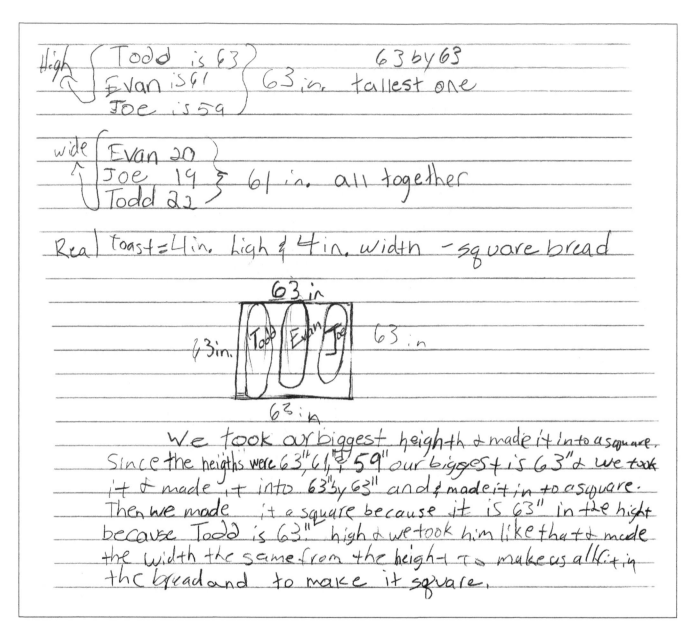

High { Todd is 63 } 63 by 63
{ Evan is 61 } 63 in. tallest one
Joe is 59

wide { Evan 20 }
{ Joe 19 } 61 in. all together
{ Todd 22 }

Real toast = 4 in. high & 4 in. width - square bread

We took our biggest heighth & made it into a square.
Since the heights were 63", 61", & 59" our biggest is 63" & we took
it & made it into 63" by 63" and & made it in to a square.
Then we made it a square because it is 63" in the hight
because Todd is 63" high & we took him like that & made
the width the same from the height To make us all fit in
the bread and to make it square.

Figure 8–1: Todd, Evan, and Joe used their measurements to create a square piece of bread modeled after their actual piece of bread.

Follow-up Problems

Once students outlined their pieces of toast with tape on the floor, I had the group of three lie down on their toast outline to show that they all fit. Next, I posed two other problems:

1. *Determine how much bigger the giant's toast is than a regular piece of toast.*
2. *Based on the relationship you found between the two pieces of toast, determine how thick the giant's toast should be.*

I intentionally made the first problem vague so it would be open to interpretation. This enabled students to solve it in different ways. Some focused on the relationship between the dimensions of an actual piece of bread and their giant toast. For example, one group had a piece of square toast that measured approximately 5 inches on a side. Their giant toast measured approximately 65 inches on a side. They divided sixty-five by five to figure out that the giant toast was thirteen times bigger than a piece of actual toast. However, others figured the area of the piece of actual toast (25 square inches), then the area of the giant's piece of toast (4,225 square inches), and compared these by dividing to decide that the giant's toast was 169 times bigger. This led to an interesting discussion about comparing areas. I asked all students to justify their answers by explaining in writing the methods they used.

Students used the relationships they had reported for the first problem to find their answers to the second problem. For example, the group that decided that the giant's toast was thirteen times bigger measured the thickness of the actual bread, found it to be about half an inch thick, and multiplied by thirteen to determine that the giant's toast would need to be $6\frac{1}{2}$ inches thick! To help put into perspective how thick the giant's toast would be, they cut a piece of tape this long and taped it vertically on a wall.

Students worked well in their groups and improved their proportional reasoning skills and strategies. They will never look at a piece of toast the same way again!

One Inch Tall

"One Inch Tall," in Shel Silverstein's *Where the Sidewalk Ends* (1974), is a poem about what life would be like if you were 1 inch tall. The poem describes how large items such as a cake crumb would seem and how you would compare with a flea.

In this lesson, students cut a piece of string the length of their height and use it to represent 1 inch. Students fold their string in half three times, using masking tape to mark off first where one-half of their "inch" would be, then the fourths, and finally the eighths. Students use this string to measure objects in the room to the nearest eighth of their string (or eighth of an "inch"). Students then use the measurements to find the proportional relationship between the size of the objects to the students' heights if they were 1 inch tall and the objects to the students' heights in real life. To do this lesson, students need to know how to find fractional parts of numbers.

MATERIALS

string, 1 6-foot piece per student

One Inch Tall **record sheet,** 1 per student (see Blackline Masters)

yardsticks, 1 per student

Introducing the Investigation

I began by reading the poem aloud and then discussing with the students in this class how the things around us would look if we were one inch tall. Then I told my students to imagine that they were one inch tall and that the entire room had shrunk in proportion with them.

"What does *proportional* mean?" I asked.

"It's like comparing two things, and then if you shrink them, they still compare the same way," Chelsey answered.

"How about an example?" I suggested.

"OK, the height of my desk is about half of my height right now. If I shrank to be an inch tall, it would shrink and still be half of my height," she explained.

I asked them to estimate, using fractions of an inch, how wide they thought their desks would be if they were one inch tall. Next I asked them to estimate the length of a sheet of paper and the height of a chair. After hearing several responses for each question, I asked students to tell me what the estimates had in common. After some discussion, we came to a consensus that all of the items would be less than an inch, as students stated, they'd all be "a fraction of an inch."

Next, I had each student cut his or her six-foot string into a piece equal to his or her height. I told the students to imagine that their string was one inch long. I had them fold a piece of tape over each end and label one end *0* and the other end *1*. I asked them how they could determine where $\frac{1}{2}$ would be. A student suggested that we fold the string in half to find the middle. This is what we did, again folding a piece of masking tape over the string and labeling it $\frac{1}{2}$. We continued folding the string to locate $\frac{1}{4}$ and $\frac{3}{4}$, and then $\frac{1}{8}, \frac{3}{8}, \frac{5}{8}$, and $\frac{7}{8}$, marking each with a piece of tape that was labeled with the appropriate fractional value.

Once they had folded and labeled their strings, I told them they were now going to use them as a ruler for measuring the objects in the "shrunken" room to the nearest eighth of an inch. In pairs and triads, students used their own string to measure items around the room and recorded their data on their *One Inch Tall* record sheets (see Blackline Masters).

When they were finished, I presented them with a challenge: "Determine if the measurements on your list would be accurate if the items were changed back to their original size. Using your measurements of the items on your list, your height if you were one inch tall, as well as your actual height, figure out the size of these items in real life."

Observing the Students

Students were stumped on how to begin this task. Several groups asked if they could use a yardstick, and I told them that they were to figure without any measuring devices. One boy took off his shoe and measured his desk. When I asked him to explain his strategy, he said, "I know my shoe is twelve inches, so I am using it to measure the desk. It's a little more than two of my shoes long, so it must be about two feet one inch or twenty-five inches." I told him it was a creative idea but reminded him that he was not allowed to use anything other than the measurement he had from using the string ruler.

Toby, Brett, and Kris were struggling with how to get started. I wanted them to think about the problem using a specific object, so I chose the height of a chair. As each of the students held their string against the thirty-inch chair it came out to about half an inch as measured by their string ruler. I chose the chair to begin with because I knew it would be approximately half an inch regardless of the string ruler used to measure it. Even though the height of the students varied as much as six inches, their string ruler still measured the chair to be approximately half an inch. I expected this because six inches represented less than one-eighth of the giant inch, so in many cases when students rounded to the nearest eighth of an inch the measurements were the same. For example, Kris who is 58″, Toby who is 61″, and Brett who is 64″ each found the height of the 30″ chair to be half of the giant inch. When they reversed the process and were asked to find the actual height of the chair, they found half of their own height. Therefore, the *estimated real measurement* for the height of the chair varied based on the student height. In this case, it was 29″ according to Kris, 30″ according to Toby, and 32″ according to Brett. An eighth of Kris's giant inch on his string ruler represented 7″ in real life; Toby's eighth of an inch on his string represented $7\frac{5}{8}$″; and Brett's represented 8″.

To help the students better understand this, I asked for the actual height of one member of the group. Toby reported that his height was sixty-one inches. I said, "If you were one inch tall, then your chair would be one-half of an inch tall. You are sixty-one inches tall. How can you use this information to find the actual height of the chair?"

"That's easy, just divide my height, sixty-one inches, by two," he replied.

"Yes, you used the proportional relationship between your height and the object when you were an inch tall compared with your actual height and the actual height of the object. What do you estimate the height of the actual chair to be?" I asked.

"It will be about thirty and one-half inches," he answered.

"Will all the members of this group come up with this same prediction?" I asked.

"I guess not, now that I think about it, because if we take half of our height and we are all different heights then we will get different predictions," Brett responded.

"Will your estimations for the real object be close?" I probed.

They thought about this for about a minute and then Kris responded, "The biggest difference will be between Brett and me because I would get twenty-nine inches and he would get thirty-two."

"How can that happen if you both thought it would be the same measurement using your string ruler?" I asked.

Kris went on to explain, "That's because we rounded. The chair was really a little more than one-half of my string, but it was close. Brett's was a little less than half of his string ruler, but rounded to one-half."

They seemed to have a good idea of what to do from here so I moved to the next group. Tammy, Sue, and Melissa were discussing the length of the desk when I joined them.

"We all got three-eighths of an inch for the length of the desk but now we are not really sure what to do," Tammy announced.

"How did you determine the actual height of the chair?" I asked, noticing that they had calculated this already.

"We just divided our actual height in half," explained Melissa.

"What can you do to find an eighth of your actual height?" I inquired.

"We can divide our actual height by eight," answered Sue.

"But we need three-eighths," interrupted Melissa.

"We can multiply by three after we divide to get the three-eighths," explained Sue. "I'm sixty inches so we can divide sixty by eight and then multiply that answer by three."

"I'm five feet and four inches. Five times twelve is sixty inches plus four more make me sixty-four inches," Tammy calculated aloud.

"Hey, that's a good one!" Melissa responded enthusiastically. "We can divide sixty-four by eight evenly!"

"One-eighth of your height would be eight inches. We need three eighths, so the length of the desk would be twenty-four inches in real life," Sue stated.

"Would each of you have the same prediction if you use your own string ruler and your own height?" I asked.

"Yes, because we all measured with our string ruler and got three-eighths of an inch," Tammy explained.

"No," said Melissa after thinking for a few seconds, "We have different actual heights to begin with so if we divide our heights by eight and multiply we won't get exactly the same answers."

"They will be close though," Tammy added.

"I think you should find out how close," I instructed. "Make sure that you find an estimate using each person's string and actual height."

I had a similar dialogue with the other groups. In many cases, students recognized that measuring in eighths of an inch on their string ruler would require them to divide by eight. Realizing this, most groups looked for a member with a height easily divisible by eight. By doing this they made the division friendly, but they ignored other possible estimates for the actual object. This is why I had each member

Figure 9–1: Lisa recorded the measurement estimates to the nearest eighth of an inch using her string ruler. She determined what the actual measurements should be in real life and listed those in the second column. She also measured in real life and recorded those measurements in the third column.

If you were 1 inch tall, how big would this be . . .

A. Use your 1-inch measuring string (to the nearest eighth of an inch) to find the height of these items in the classroom, assuming they shrank along with you!

B. Your task is to determine if these measurements are correct. Use your measurement from Column A and determine what the length of your desk should be in real life. You *cannot* use a ruler to measure the desk. Do this for each item below and record in Column B.

C. When you have finished with the estimations, use a real yardstick to find the actual measurements and record them in the last column. How accurate were your estimates?

$$7.5 \over 8 \overline{)60}$$

Item	A. String Measurement	B. Estimated Real Measurement	C. Real Measurement
1. Length of your desk	about ½	30 in.	24 in.
2. Length of math book	about ⅛	7.5 in.	8 in.
3. Height of your chair	about ½	30 in.	26 in
4. Width of classroom door	about ⅝	38 in.	36 in.
5. Height of bookshelf/ closet door	about 1¼	75 in.	84 in
6. Width of a window	about 4/8	30 in.	36 in.
7. Length of your pencil	about ⅛	7.5 in.	48 in.
8. Height of garbage can	about 2/8	15 in.	8 in.
9. Item of your choice: depth of sink	about ⅛	7.5 in.	6 in.
10. Item of your choice: around the globe	about 7/8	52.5 in	18 in.

Our string ruler is 1 inch and there is 12 inches in a foot. The answer above ~~the desk~~ is 1/2", so it would be one half of us which would be 2½ ft. (I am 5 ft.)

find their estimate so that the students could see the range of estimated real measurements. Once started, they were able to determine the size of the items in real life for each of them with relative ease.

As the final step, I had them use yardsticks to measure the actual size of the items to check the accuracy of their solutions. They were

Math and Literature, Grades 6–8

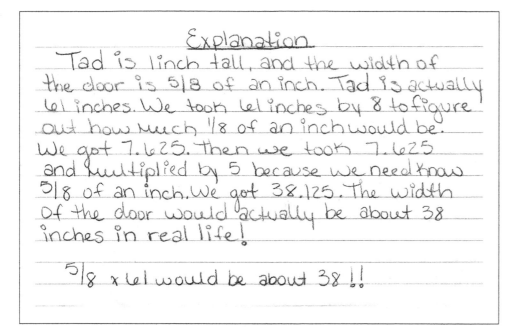

Explanation

Tad is 1 inch tall, and the width of the door is 5/8 of an inch. Tad is actually 61 inches. We took 61 inches by 8 to figure out how much 1/8 of an inch would be. We got 7.625. Then we took 7.625 and multiplied by 5 because we need know 5/8 of an inch. We got 38.125. The width of the door would actually be about 38 inches in real life!

5/8 x 61 would be about 38 !!

Figure 9–2: Courtney explained how she determined the size of an object in real life that measured $\frac{5}{8}$ of her string ruler. She used division to find how much $\frac{1}{8}$ of an inch on her string ruler would be in real life. She then used multiplication to determine how much $\frac{5}{8}$ of an inch would be.

excited to see how close many of their measurements actually were. We also had a discussion about why we came up with a range of estimated real measurements when using our string rulers to predict. We then talked about adding sixteenths to the ruler, which would have made the measurements using the string ruler different in some cases (depending on the height of the student) and also would have made the "estimated real measurements" predicted by each student using their string ruler more accurate.

The hands-on nature of this activity was inviting to the students and maintained their attention and enthusiasm througout the lesson.

Shapes

"Shapes" is a short poem from *A Light in the Attic*, by Shel Silverstein (1981). In this poem, a square is injured by a falling triangle. A circle that is rolling by picks them up and takes them to the hospital.

During this lesson, students explore the relationship between the circumference and the diameter of a circle and develop an understanding of the meaning of pi. Students use the diameter of a circle to find its circumference and use this information in a problem-solving situation to determine the number of rolls it would take a circle of a given size to roll a specified distance.

MATERIALS

cardboard circles of various sizes, such as 6-inch, 8-inch,10-inch,12-inch diameters, with a hole punched out in the center large enough for a pencil to fit through, 4 per group (group size: two to four students)

Shapes **worksheet,** 1 per student (see Blackline Masters)

tape measure, 1 per group

rulers, 1 per student

string, 1 per group

Introducing the Investigation

Because my students did not have a good understanding of what pi was and how it related to diameter and circumference, I spent a day prior to introducing the poem having students explore the relationship between circumference and diameter to develop the concept of pi (Day 1 of this lesson). Depending on the experiences of your students, you may choose to start with Day 1 or Day 2.

Day 1

I gave each group of students four cardboard circles of various sizes and asked them to find a relationship between the circumference and the diameter of a circle.

"What do you need to know in order to complete this task?" I asked.

"We need to know what the circumference and diameter are," Tom answered.

"What parts of the circle are they?" I asked.

"The circumference is the distance around the circle, like the perimeter of a rectangle, only circumference goes with circles," Sally responded.

"What about the diameter?" I questioned.

Sally continued, "It's the distance across the circle from one side to the other, but you have to go through the center."

"What do you think I mean when I ask for a relationship between the circumference and the diameter?" I asked.

Kim replied, "You mean you want to know how they go together."

"What pattern is there between them," Jonathan added.

"I've made a chart for you to record the circumference and the diameter of the circles so that you can look for a relationship," I explained. "You have four circles in your group to work with. You'll need to be sure you measure very accurately."

I distributed the *Shapes* worksheet, which had columns for circumference, diameter, and the ratio of circumference to diameter (see Blackline Masters). Using rulers and measuring tapes, students began measuring and recording. Students wrote the ratios in different ways. Some used a colon, some a fraction, and others wrote it as a decimal.

"What do you notice about the relationship between the circumference and the diameter?" I asked.

"The circumference is always bigger than the diameter, for one thing," answered Phillip.

"Which ratio format makes it easiest to look for patterns?" I asked.

Using a calculator to change his fraction to a decimal, Phillip said, "I guess the decimal does because it is simplified that way. My fractions are too complicated, like eighteen over five point five. If I just divide it, I get, ummm, about three point two seven. That's an easier number."

"OK, but what does that mean in terms of the relationship between circumference and diameter?" I questioned.

"It means that it takes about three circumferences to equal a diameter. No wait, it's the other way around because the diameter is smaller than the circumference."

"Do all of the circles have that relationship? Take a few minutes to check your data," I instructed.

After a few minutes I asked, "What do you think? Do you see any patterns?"

"They are all around three," Tammy answered.

"Yah, we got that too," Phillip replied.

"Who remembers what pi is?" I asked.

"It's a number that doesn't end, I remember that," Tammy replied.

"It's the number of diameters it would take to make the circumference of any circle," Phillip answered.

"Any size circle?" I probed.

"Yes, any size," Phillip responded.

"So it works for the pupil of my eye and a big garbage can?" Dan asked.

"Look at the four circles you experimented with in your task. Were they all about the same ratio even though they were different sizes?" I asked.

"Looks like it," Dan answered.

Class had nearly ended, so for homework I asked each student to write down everything he or she knew about diameter and circumference. I explained that the students would need this information for the next day's activity.

Day 2

On the second day I started class by having students share what they had written about circumference for homework with their groups so everybody would have a chance to speak. I then asked three students to share their written responses with the whole class. (See Figure 10–1 for David's response.) I reminded them that this information would be helpful in solving today's task.

Then I read aloud the poem "Shapes." On the floor on one side of the room, I had taped a square labeled *home,* and on the other side of the room, I'd taped another square labeled *hospital,* with a "road" (strip of masking tape) between the two. I pointed this out to the class. I gave each group a different-sized cardboard circle and a ruler, then asked the students to figure out how many rolls it would take for their circles to get from home to the hospital. First, they talked in their groups about what they would need to know to solve this problem and then we discussed the question as a whole class. Students realized they would need to know the circumference of the circle and the distance to the hospital. I laid a tape measure on the floor, stretched from home to the hospital, so they could find the distance

Circle Number	Circumference	Diameter	Ratio of C to D
1	9 cm	3 cm	3 cm
2	44½ cm	14 cm	3.17
3	15 cm	5	3 cm
4	55 cm	17	3.27 cm
Average			3.1

There is a way to measure circumfrance around a circle
With out using string. What you do is First measure the
diameter in the shape. π (pi) is 3 distances or almost 3 distances
around a circle (π is always about 3 diameters around a circle). So sec.
you take the diameter mutiplied by π (3). Also if you are
wanting to know the diameter of something than take
your circumfrance divided by π (3).

① ex: ① ⊘ diameter 8 in.   ② 8 × π (3) = 24   ③ circumfrance is 24 in.

② ex: ⊘ circumfrance = 15 in   ② (3)π)15̄ −15 / 0   ③ the diameter is 5

(these are estimates)

Figure 10–1: David recorded his data in the table and explained his understanding of pi.

between the two. I asked students to use only rulers to measure their circles, so they could measure only the diameter for each circle and had to use that information to determine the circumference.

One group had a hard time determining what to do with its measurements for diameter and circumference. The kids tried drawing a picture and imagining that they were "unwinding" the circumference of the circle along the tape measure. This was hard for them to visualize, so I suggested they cut a string the length of the circumference. Then I started at home and laid the string next to the tape measure. I asked them if this was long enough to reach the hospital. They could see that clearly, it was not. I asked them how we could determine how many strings of that size it would take. First, they suggested that I mark where the string ended and then move it so that it started at that point on the tape measure. If I continued to do this, they explained, I would be able to count how many strings it would take. I agreed that this idea would work and asked them how they could do this numerically if the string couldn't be moved. They determined that they would need to know how many string lengths (the circumference) there were in the distance to the hospital. They returned to their table to work out the calculations.

Once the groups determined the number of rolls they thought it would take to get from home to the hospital, I explained how they were to check their results. I showed them how to mark a starting point on the circumference of their circle and put a pencil through the center of the circle. Holding each end of the pencil, they could start at home with the mark pointed down at the floor and roll the circle to the hospital. Each time the mark went around and hit the floor, they counted it as a roll. They stopped counting when they reached the hospital. It was apparent by their surprise that some students did not completely understand what they were finding until they rolled their circles from home to the hospital. At that point, they had an "ah-ha" moment and really understood what they were doing and how the circumference was really an integral part of this task. Also, when they finished their route to the hospital, if the circle had gone only a fraction of the way around, students had to estimate what part of the circumference had been rolled in the final roll.

In the end, students compared the results of rolling the circle with the mental calculations they'd done earlier. The discussion that followed enabled the students to explain that the circumference is a linear measurement and involves measuring the distance around the circle. What makes this difficult and hard to imagine is the fact that the length is curved to form a circle; wrapping string around the circle, then removing the string and stretching it out to form a line better enables students to visualize the circumference in one dimension.

Students enjoyed this lesson and referred back to it later in the year when discussing circumference.

Shipwreck at the Bottom
of the World

*The Extraordinary True Story of
Shackelton and the* Endurance

Jennifer Armstrong's novel *Shipwreck at the Bottom of the World* (1998) is about Ernest Shackelton and the twenty-seven men who, in 1921, set out to become the first team to cross Antarctica. Instead of reaching their destination, their ship, the *Endurance*, became trapped in ice and ultimately sank. The story follows the crew's treacherous journey across ice flocs and wild seas to an island where twenty-two of the men made camp. The other six men traversed 800 miles of stormy ocean to find a rescue ship. In the end, all twenty-eight men survived! *Shipwreck* offers opportunities to explore estimation, measurement, mapping, and time lines, as well to make connections to other disciplines.

This lesson includes two investigations. Students first estimate and then measure various distances to develop a sense of large linear measurements. In a second investigation, students create a time line of the expedition's events and figure out the fractional amount of the total expedition that has passed when each event occurs. This is an excellent opportunity for students to explore fractions of a length (a time line), rather than fractions of an area, which is much more common.

MATERIALS

rulers, yardsticks, or tape measures, 1 per student

adding machine paper strips, about 2.5 feet long, for time lines, 1 per student

transparency of map from *Shipwreck at the Bottom of the World*

Important Dates of the Endurance *Expedition,* 1 per student (see Blackline Masters)

Introducing the Investigation

All I needed to capture the attention of the class was to read aloud the first paragraph of Chapter 1 from *Shipwreck at the Bottom of the World*. I then asked the students what they knew about conditions in Antarctica: "How low do you think temperatures sink in Antarctica?" Students thought for a moment and then shared their predictions.

Kyle said, "Minus ten degrees. Nowhere could get colder than that."

Robin guessed, "I think it can get lots colder. I'd say minus fifty degrees."

Next I asked, "How fast do you think the winds could blow?"

Students predicted between 50 and 300 miles per hour.

Next, I asked the students, "How cold do you ever remember it being in Kansas?" Students agreed that the coldest it got was just a few degrees below zero.

Finally, I asked students how big they thought the area of ice in Antarctica in the winter was compared with the area of something in their own experience (e.g., the area of their town, their state, the United States).

After discussing their predictions, I read the second paragraph of the opening chapter, which revealed that temperatures could drop to −100 degrees and winds could blow as much as 200 miles per hour.

"Wow, how did they stay alive?" Conner asked. "They couldn't have had very good coats and gloves in those days." This led to a discussion about fabrics and current technology in cold-weather protection. Students who had predicted the wind speed at 200 miles per hour were excited to share the reasoning behind their estimates. Sarah said, "When we had seventy-mile winds in town, it tore branches off the trees. What would two hundred-mile-per-hour winds be like?"

The second paragraph also states that the frozen sea reaches an area of 7 million square miles. I asked the students, "How does this area compare with that of the United States?"

Amanda guessed that it was about half the size of the United States while Christian said, "I bet it's about the size of Alaska." All were surprised to find out it was twice the size of the entire United States. Marilyn volunteered to get the globe and find Antarctica for us. As she pointed on the globe to Antarctica, I showed a transparency from a map in the book that showed the crew's travels from Argentina to Antarctica.

After this introductory discussion of the journey, we began a measurement exploration. Much of the story discusses various linear measurements (length of the boat, the distance traveled, etc.) and therefore offers an opportunity for students to estimate with length and develop benchmarks. I read the introduction to the book and the first few pages of Chapter 2, which describe the ship. The *Endurance* was 144 feet long and 25 feet wide with a hull "in some places more than four feet thick." I asked students to try to envision how big this ship was compared with our classroom or school. I explained to them that we were going to estimate and then measure each one of the ship's dimensions. First I asked them to line up in pairs, with pairs facing each other and standing 4 feet apart. Estimations of 4 feet varied greatly, so we placed yardsticks between students to help them picture a 4-foot-thick hull.

We then went into the hallway. I chose two volunteers to help me measure, then I said, "I'd like the rest of you to walk down the hall and stop whenever you think you are twenty-five feet from me. This is the width of the ship." When each student was satisfied with his or her estimate, Nikki and Emily used a tape measure to mark 25 feet. Tom was especially excited to find that he had estimated nearly perfectly. Other students, who had not estimated as well, did a much better job when we repeated this process for the length of the ship. They used their newly formed ideas of how long 25 feet was and even discussed how many 25s would be in 144. After seeing the ship's measurements, Stacy exclaimed, "That would be really cramped for twenty-eight men and all of the supplies and sixty-nine sled dogs! I can't believe that they all fit in there."

We went back to the classroom to work on a few more activities, including estimating and then measuring the length of the 11-foot leopard seal that tried to kill a crew member, the 15-inch ice that encased the small boats, and the 100-foot waves that almost capsized them. Amy noted, "It would take one of our fifty-foot tape measures and both of our twenty-five-foot tape measures to measure a wave that high!"

We also discussed the 2,000-pound lifeboats the crew used. I asked the students to identify an object from their own lives that would help us understand how heavy 2000 pounds was.

Nikki said, "Wouldn't that be about as much as your VW Bug?"

Brian said, "I think it would be about twenty people because we each weigh about a hundred pounds."

It was clear that the estimates and comparisons we discussed enabled students to make sense of the large numbers they heard in the story. Merry pointed out, "Isn't eight hundred miles [the record number of miles traveled by a lifeboat over a winter ocean] about twice as far as it is across Kansas? Wow!"

A Follow-up Activity

As a second investigation, we created time lines of the events that occurred over the two-year adventure. We used the information on the time line to discuss fraction concepts, in particular finding common fractions to describe the approximate time of the total expedition that had passed at several key dates during the adventure. I handed out 2.5-foot strips of adding machine tape to the students. Students used rulers to create their own time lines with twenty-five equally spaced slash marks that they labeled with each of the twenty-five months of the expedition (from August 1914 to August 1916).

I sketched a time line on the chalkboard and distributed *Important Dates of the* Endurance *Expedition* (see Blackline Masters). (These dates can be found in the book in Chapter 3 and on the map in the front of the book.) As a class, we started by placing the day the *Endurance* was crushed by ice—October 27, 1915—on our time lines. I asked the class what fraction of the total expedition time the crew had passed when this happened. Students struggled to come up with a fraction to describe the relative time that had passed.

Janet counted twenty-five total months on the time line and noticed that the crew abandoned ship at the end of the fourteenth month.

"Fifteen out of twenty-five would be a friendlier fraction," Stacy said. "That would be about three-fifths of the time of the trip."

Cheryl said, "I did it differently. I folded my time line and saw that it was a little over half the time, so I said it was six-tenths."

Kyle said, "I thought about the trip as two years long, so fourteen months was over a year, so I knew it was more than half. But it wasn't a year and a half, so somewhere between that. So, I just said it was five-eighths."

I asked the class, "Can these different estimates all be correct?"

Emily asked, "Well, isn't Cheryl's answer the same as Stacy's because sixth-tenths simplifies to three-fifths?"

"What about Kyle's estimate?" I asked.

"It's different," Nikki responded.

I paused briefly and then asked the class, "Can the two estimates be acceptable?"

Students discussed the question, pointing out that one might be closer to the right answer, but both of the fractions were close to $\frac{14}{25}$ so they were both good estimates.

I asked students to divide into groups of three so they could work together to place the other events on their number lines and record common fractions to describe about how much of the trip had passed when each event occurred.

One group tried to find where to place the May 10 landing on South Georgia Island. Rauol said, "I think the mark should go here [pointing at a line about one-third of the way from May to June] because ten is about one-third of thirty-one."

Students used various strategies for deciding the fraction of time that had passed. Some folded their time lines. Some used the fact that the trip took twenty-five months to select a common fraction to describe the fraction of the trip that had passed. Others marked some common fractions underneath their number lines, such as fourths, eighths, sixths, and tenths, and used these as guides to find a common fraction to describe the part of the trip that had been completed.

As students estimated and measured, discussed temperatures, wind speed, linear measurements, weight, and time, and compared adventures of the *Endurance* crew with their own personal experience, they deepened their understanding of measurement concepts, such as developing benchmarks and calculating fractions in a linear model, as well as their knowledge about Antarctica.

Spaghetti and Meatballs for All!

In Marilyn Burns's *Spaghetti and Meatballs for All!* (1997), Mr. and Mrs. Comfort decide to have the family over for a feast. Thirty-two family members respond that they can come. Mrs. Comfort figures that eight square tables will seat everyone. As guests arrive, they begin pushing tables together to be closer to each other, reducing the number of available seats. Soon, they have to begin pulling the tables apart to make room for more people, and eventually they get back to the original plan of eight separate tables, each seating four.

This story provides a context for exploring relationships between area and perimeter. Students often confuse perimeter and area and sometimes think that if different rectangles have the same area, they also have the same perimeter. In this lesson, students first explore shapes that have a constant area but a changing perimeter. Then they create shapes with a constant perimeter and changing area. Students also begin developing notions of how to maximize or minimize area, given a set perimeter, and vice versa.

MATERIALS

color tiles, about 50 per pair of students

centimeter-squared paper, 2–3 sheets per student (see Blackline Masters)

Introducing the Investigation

I asked the students to come to the front of the room and sit on the floor for a math lesson. I began the lesson by reading aloud *Spaghetti and Meatballs for All!*

The entire class was intrigued by the story, eager to hear about the math investigation. I asked the class for some comments about what had happened in the story. Leslie said, "The tables ended like Mrs. Comfort had originally planned them!"

Candice agreed. "Yeah, why didn't they just keep the tables where they were in the first place?"

"Because people wanted to sit together," Landran answered.

"Yeah, and it takes one away from each table when you put them together," Joanna explained.

Anthony disagreed. "No, there's four sides to a table and you take away two sides of the tables when you put them together." The class agreed with Anthony.

I asked the students to return to their tables and work with their table partners on an investigation. I gave each pair a set of about fifty color tiles. As I passed out the tiles, I asked, "How many people were the Comforts expecting?"

"Thirty-two!" the students replied.

"Right, and how many tables had Mrs. Comfort ordered for the party?"

"Eight!" the class responded.

"Right. Now, I need you to take eight tiles to represent the eight tables and arrange them on your desk the way that Mrs. Comfort originally arranged them—all separate, not together," I directed. "Now, the combined area of these tiles is what?"

Jasmine answered, "Eight tiles."

I said, "What is the combined perimeter?" When I noticed that I was getting some blank stares, I took a step back and asked, "What does *perimeter* mean?"

"It's the distance around, right?" Jessie ventured.

"That's correct. So what's the perimeter of one tile?"

Katie answered, "Four."

Then I asked, "And the perimeter of two separate squares is what?"

"Eight," Leslie responded.

"Yes, and for all eight tiles, what's the perimeter?"

"Thirty-two!" Aaron exclaimed.

"All right, now let's push two tables together and see what happens. Has the area changed?"

"Yes, because if the tables are connected, it takes away two sides," Mica explained.

"But there are still eight tiles," argued Mackenna.

Several students pointed out that the area had not changed, but the perimeter had changed.

"Can somebody explain why the area hasn't changed?" I asked.

"Because if you take a big piece of carpet and cut it up and then put the pieces back together, they will still take up the same amount of space," Katie explained.

"Now, think about whether or not the total perimeter has changed. Use your tiles to figure the perimeter. Think about if you put a chair on each side, how many chairs can you use?" I prompted. After a couple of minutes, students were ready to share.

"The perimeter is now only thirty," Candice stated.

"Did anyone else come up with something different?" I asked.

"Yeah, I came up with twenty-eight," answered Jennet.

"What do the rest of you think? Can someone explain to us how you came up with your answer?" I asked the class.

Abby raised her hand and explained, "I have the six tables that are still by themselves over here [pointing at the six tiles] so that makes twenty-four seats. These combined tables can seat six more people. So twenty-four and six is thirty."

I turned to the class and said, "Do you agree with Abby's answer?"

Miguel jumped in and said, "I agree, but I did it differently. I knew that at the start, the tables were for thirty-two people and that two were lost by pushing them together, so take away two and you get thirty."

I responded, "Does anyone else have a different way to explain?" No one volunteered, so I asked students to move on to the next step. "OK, next they pushed two more tables together, right? Does it matter how we push these two tables together with the two already pushed together?" I asked.

"Yes," Anthony stated, "because if you put them in a square, you take away more chairs than just a line of tables."

"OK, in the book they made a square with the four tables. So, take four tiles and arrange them in a square, and leave the other four unconnected. Now, has the area changed?" I asked.

"No, we still have eight tiles," Joanna replied.

"And what is the perimeter now?" I asked.

"Twenty-four," Leslie answered, "because there are four tables with four sides, which is sixteen, and then the big table made from pushing four tables together has another eight."

"What if the tables were added in a row instead? How would the perimeter change?" I asked.

Landran said, "It would be more because there aren't as many sides in the middle."

"Let's find out. Build the four tables in a row and find the perimeter." After several minutes of working, students had built the new arrangement and had found the perimeter.

"What's the perimeter with the tables in this arrangement?" I asked.

"It went up by two to twenty-six!" Blaine exclaimed.

"So it really does matter how you arrange the tables, doesn't it?" The class agreed, and I continued. "Next in the book, they pushed two more tables into the square of four to make a new rectangle. I think the area will still be the same; what do you think will happen to the perimeter?"

"It will get smaller," Nate said.

"Yeah, the perimeter is now only eighteen," Jennet agreed.

Students built the next table formation from the book and confirmed that it did have a perimeter of eighteen. We continued this through the last combination of tables. Then we discussed perimeter.

"Does it really matter how the tables are arranged?" I asked.

"Yes, because every time you change the arrangement, the perimeter changes, too," Joanna explained.

"The more you push the tables together, the fewer places you have for people to sit," Candice added.

Anthony elaborated, saying, "If you push the tables together in a fat rectangle or like a square, then it would have the smallest perimeter. If you want a lot of perimeter, you have to spread out the tables."

A Follow-up Problem

"Keep this in mind as we move to our next problem. We know that there are thirty-two people coming to dinner. Besides the arrangement that Mrs. Comfort designed, please arrange your tiles in as many different ways as you can that will seat thirty-two people—in other words, ways that will have a perimeter of thirty-two. You can change the area as much as you want. You can use more than eight tiles as long as each of your arrangements has a perimeter of thirty-two. You can put as many tables together or keep as many separate as you want as long as the perimeter is thirty-two," I instructed. "Record each new way on your centimeter-squared paper."

As the students began working, I circulated around the room. Anthony and Jessie explained their design to me, which was four groups of four tables: "If you have four groups of four tables, that's thirty-two because you can seat eight people at each group of tables and there are four groups. Eight times four is thirty-two!" They were very excited about their design and their explanation. (See Figure 12–1.)

Leslie and Candice explained how they found their design of a long row of tables: "We counted four people at each table but had to take away two people every time we added a table, except for the ends because three people can sit at the tables at the end. So, every

Figure 12–1: Jesse and Anthony's seating arrangement had sixteen color tiles.

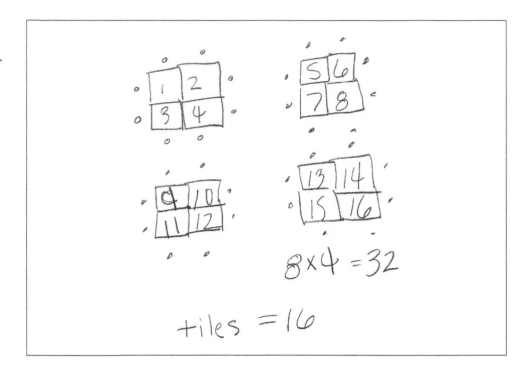

Figure 12–2: Leslie and Candice created a different arrangement.

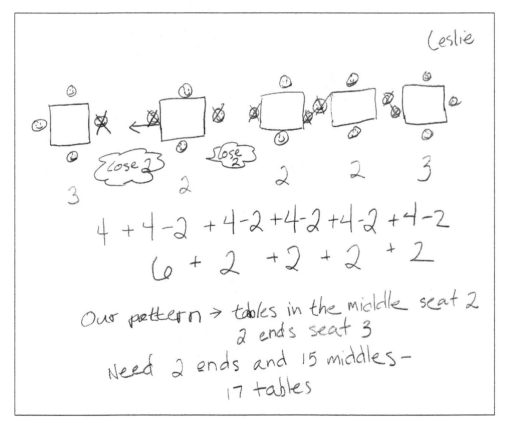

time we added a table, we had to subtract two where the tables connected." (See Figure 12–2.)

Blaine and Nate had placed their tiles in a long row so that sides didn't touch, but the corners did. They explained, "See, four people can still sit at each table if you just connect the corners together!"

Math and Literature, Grades 6–8

After about five minutes, I asked for their attention, as it became clear to me that each group was focusing on only one arrangement. "Be sure to consider different arrangements. For example, what about groups of two or three tables? Try to think beyond a line of tables or individual tables."

Nate asked, "Could you make a hollow square and have people sitting inside?"

I responded, "How would you get those people to the inside of the square?"

"Oh yeah," he replied.

"It's a good idea," I pushed. "Is there a way you can adjust it so that people can get in and out?"

"Hey, yeah, like a U shape!" he exclaimed and immediately went to work conjuring up a new arrangement of tables.

A Class Discussion

After about ten minutes, I called the students together as a whole class and asked them to explain the shapes they came up with and each shape's area and perimeter. There were varying shapes and areas ranging from fifteen tiles to forty-two tiles.

"OK, now that some of us have shared our new designs, why do you think that Mrs. Comfort ordered only eight tables?"

Lauren suggested, "Because she had to rent them and she probably didn't want to pay for a whole bunch of tables."

"What do you suppose is the smallest number of tables you would need to use to get a perimeter of thirty-two?"

"Eight," Landran answered.

"Because . . . ?" I prompted.

"Because the most people you can have at a table is four, and eight times four is thirty-two," he explained.

To bring the lesson to a close, I asked the following: "What relationships did you notice between perimeter and area? Talk to your partner and I will ask you to report in a few minutes." When it was time to share, students had some interesting observations.

MacKenna said, "Perimeter goes around the outside of a shape, and area is the inside part. If the shape is real long or spread out, the perimeter can be really big, but if the area is all squished together, the perimeter is less."

"You can have an area that is bigger than a perimeter and vice versa," Mica stated.

"If you have a certain table arrangement and you want to make room for more people, you need to spread out the tables more," Nate explained. "The most perimeter you will get is if the area is all separate."

Jessie said, "Yeah, and if you want to have a lot of area and not much perimeter, then you want to push it all together, like in a square."

"What I hear you saying is that if you want a lot of perimeter, then you want a shape that's spread out, and if you want to minimize the perimeter, you want to make the shape as square as you can. What do the rest of you think about that?"

"I agree," Candice said. "That is why Mrs. Comfort wanted the most spread-out arrangement."

Landran added, "And in our designs, the most squarish one used the most tiles to sit thirty-two people."

The class was engaged for the duration of the lesson and learned important concepts about area and perimeter. The language they used and the explanations they offered demonstrated a conceptual understanding of perimeter and area and a strong understanding of the relationships between the two.

Tikki Tikki Tembo

Arlene Mosel's book *Tikki Tikki Tembo* (1968) revolves around a boy with a very long name: Tikki tikki tembo-no sa rembo-chari bari ruchi-pip peri pembo. When the boy falls into a deep well, his brother, Chang, runs for help. It takes Chang so long to say his brother's name when calling for help that he nearly drowns. The moral to the story is that short names are better than long ones.

This story leads into an investigation of "average." Students create a human box-and-whisker plot as well as one on graphing calculators, interpret the information they collect, and develop a better understanding of mean, median, and mode. This lesson spans three class periods.

MATERIALS

Day 1

cubes or counters, about 15 per student

2-by-2-inch pieces of paper, 1 per student

ball of yarn or string

perforated computer paper, about 10 to 15 sheets, not separated, or a roll of paper towels

Day 2

2-by-2-inch pieces of paper, 6 per student

6 envelopes labeled with a letter (M, E, O, B, T, A)

graphing calculators, 1 per student

$8\frac{1}{2}$-by-11-inch paper for sketching box-and-whisker plot, 1 sheet per student

Day 3

plots from the day before, posted around the room

Day 1

On the first day, I began by reading *Tikki Tikki Tembo* to the class. We first discussed the length of this character's full name. I asked that each student record on the square piece of paper the total number of letters in his or her first and last names together and take from the bucket of cubes on his or her table that number of cubes. When asked whether they should use their formal name or, if they had one, a nickname, I left the choice up to each of them.

After students had the correct number of cubes in their hands, I asked them to get out of their seats and go from student to student, exchanging the number of cubes in their hands until everyone in the class had the same number. The students could not do this exactly. Some had eleven cubes and some had twelve, and they continued passing them back and forth, but they could not get everyone to have the same number. At this point students asked me what to do because they couldn't break up the cubes to allow each student to have an equal amount. I asked them why they would want to break the cubes apart. Sue answered, "Because we are trying to split these up evenly and everyone should have a number between eleven and twelve cubes if we were going to try to divide these up equally." When the students thought they were as close as they could get to having the same number of cubes in their hands, I had them sit back down. I had them recount the number of cubes because students sometimes lose count as they move around the room. After they recounted the cubes, we quickly went around the room and every student reported the number of cubes in his or her hand. A few last-minutes changes were necessary.

I began a discussion about what the number of cubes in their hands meant. I asked the class, "What have we done with the cubes?"

"We tried to even them out," Dana answered.

"What do you mean by that?" I asked.

"Well, I mean some people had more than this," she said as she extended her hand to show her cubes, "and some people had less. Now we have the same number, or about the same. Maybe I should have said we made all of them equal or as close as we could because we couldn't break them apart."

"What do we call this number when we even it out like Dana has suggested?" I asked.

"I think she is talking about the mean," Todd answered.

Again, I asked the students what the number of cubes each of them had in their hands meant.

"They represent the number of letters in our names," Sarah said.

I then said, "Whoever has a name that is longer than the mean, raise your hand." Several students raised their hands.

Then I said, "Whoever has a name shorter than the mean, raise your hand." Other students raised their hands.

Finally I asked students who had a name equal to the class mean to raise their hands. Then I had the students return the cubes to their buckets.

I asked students if there might have been an easier way to pass the cubes out into equal groups. After several minutes of brainstorming in small groups, students shared their ideas. One group suggested that we put all of the cubes into one big group and then pass them out evenly to split them up with everyone. I asked the students what mathematical operation we would use when "putting them all into one big group." They easily identified this as addition. Then I asked them what mathematical operation we would use when "splitting them up." Again, students easily identified this as division.

I asked each of the students in a group of five to tell me the number of letters in his or her first and last names. I wrote these numbers on the board—*11, 10, 11, 11, 13*—and had the others add them and divide by 5 to determine the mean of the letters in the names of the people in that group. After dividing the sum of 56 by 5, some students reported an answer of $11\frac{1}{5}$ and others reported 11.2. I asked what this told us about the average number of letters in the names of the students in the group. We agreed that in the context of letters, 11 was a reasonable average for that group.

I directed the students in that group to again take the number of cubes equal to the number of letters in their names and had them "act out" the mean for the class. The five students began exchanging the cubes between them until four of them had eleven cubes and one had twelve. We talked about the extra cube. If everyone had eleven, the extra cube divided among them would give each person one-fifth of a cube but it wasn't possible to break a cube apart.

I asked all of the students to bring their square pieces of paper with the number of letters in their names written on them to the front of the room. I asked them to order themselves from those with the least number of letters in their names to those with the greatest. I asked the students the statistical name for the greatest number (*maximum*) and smallest number (*minimum*). Starting at each end, I had one student from each end sit down on the floor right where he or she was standing at the same time. I moved to the next two students, one on each end, and had them sit down on the floor. I continued asking students to sit down until I got to the middle of the line and the last two students were standing. Because two students were left standing rather than one, I asked the students what they thought we should do to find out the middle number. Sharon suggested finding the mean of the two numbers and the rest of the class agreed. I asked the class what the statistical name was for the person standing in the middle. Andrew answered, "Median."

"What is another meaning of the word *median*?" I asked.

"Sometimes you hear people talk about it when they are talking about driving down the road. Someone might cross the median. It is the middle part of the highway," Charlene suggested.

"So it still means middle?" I asked.

"Yes," she confirmed.

I had the students in the greater half of the group stand up again. We repeated the same procedure with just those students. I gave the name "upper quartile" to the middle student left standing in this case. I then had the students in the lesser half stand up. We repeated the procedure again with just those students. I gave the middle student standing in this case the name "lower quartile." Then I asked the students why they thought those two students might have the name "quartile."

Joe answered, "Because the quartiles split us up into four groups now instead of just two, like when you have a median."

I gave the person in the position of upper quartile one end of a piece of perforated computer paper that was attached to several other pieces. I unfolded the paper until I reached the lower quartile. Here I removed the remaining papers and gave the other end of the long banner of paper to the lower quartile to hold. I explained to the students that when we make a box-and-whisker plot, these are the terms that mark the beginning and end of the box. I then gave the upper quartile the end of a piece of string. I unwound the string until I got to the "upper extreme," or maximum value. This was the last person in the upper quartile. I cut the string and gave it to the person in the position of upper extreme to hold. I repeated this process with the lower quartile and unwound the string and gave the other end to the "lower extreme," or minimum value. I explained that in a box-and-whisker plot, the whiskers represent the values on the ends, or extremities. I then went back to the median and drew a vertical line down the paper at that position. (See Figure 13–1.)

I then gave the students some tape and had them attach each part of the box-and-whisker plot to the wall behind them. I also had them tape their small square pieces of paper with their names on them in the appropriate locations on the board so that we could refer back to this box-and-whisker plot later. (See Figure 13–2.)

Finally, before I had them sit down, I had the students separate into groups according to the number of letters in their names. I had students with no matches go back to their seats. I then asked how many students had found one other person with the same number of letters in his or her name. I asked if there were any groups larger

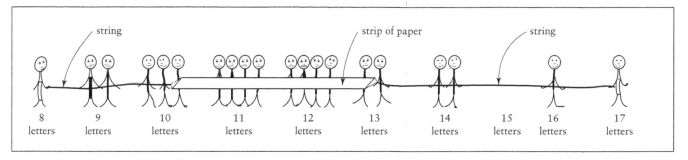

Figure 13-1: Students modeling a box-and-whisker plot for name lengths.

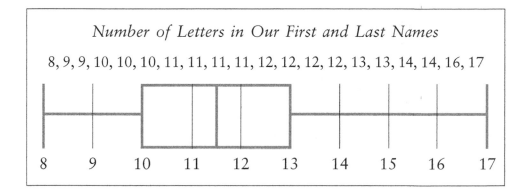

Number of Letters in Our First and Last Names

8, 9, 9, 10, 10, 10, 11, 11, 11, 11, 12, 12, 12, 12, 13, 13, 14, 14, 16, 17

8   9   10   11   12   13   14   15   16   17

Figure 13-2: Box-and-whisker plot of name lengths. This is how it looked on the wall. We added numbers, evenly spaced, in the appropriate places.

than two. There were two groups of four, so I had all the other groups go back to their seats. I then asked the class why these students were still standing at the front of the class.

"Four of them had the same number of letters in their names and the other group of four had the same number of letters in their names. That was the biggest group of people. I guess you could say they had the most popular number of letters in their names," Sue explained as the class laughed.

I asked them if they could tell me the statistical name for the number that occurs more often than the others.

"It's the mode," Josh answered quickly.

I went on to explain that if you have two sets of numbers that both occur more often then you have a situation that is *bimodal*.

I told them that we would be doing more with box-and-whisker plots in class the next day now that they had an initial understanding of what they were.

Day 2

The second day I gave the students an oral survey. I asked one question, had them write their answers on small slips of paper, and collected those slips and put them in an envelope labeled *M*. I then asked a second question and repeated the previous procedure, labeling the envelope *E*. I continued this for all six questions, so I had envelopes labeled *M, E, Q, B, T,* and *A.* (I intentionally chose letters that weren't in sequence.) I made a master list of question numbers and the corresponding envelope labels for later reference. The survey questions were as follows:

1. On average, how many minutes of TV do you watch in a week? (M)

2. How long (in minutes) is your average shower (or bath)? (E)

3. How many books do you read in a month? (Q)

4. How many years old are you? (B)

5. How many days did you go to a pool during your summer vacation? (T)

6. As far back as you can remember, how many times have you moved? (A)

I organized the class into groups of three. I gave each group an envelope, but did not tell the kids which question their data represented. I asked each group to order the numbers on the slips of paper from smallest to greatest. I then asked each group to record these numbers on a piece of paper in case the slips were lost as class progressed. (I learned that I needed to take this precaution the hard way the first time I tried this activity!) The groups would also need this list to enter the data into their graphing calculators.

I passed out graphing calculators to all students. We went through the steps of clearing the data from the memory. Then I gave them instructions on how to enter a list of numbers into the calculator. After all students entered the list that their group had made using the data in their envelope collected from the class, I had them use the "stat plot" key on the graphing calculator and select a box-and-whisker plot from this data. Students helped each other through this process. If a student got lost, I had him or her set the calculator down and look on with another member of the group. When we finished, each group had at least one box-and-whisker plot for its data. I directed the students to use the "trace" key to find the median, upper quartile, lower quartile, minimum, and maximum. I then instructed them to make a sketch of this plot on $8\frac{1}{2}$-by-11-inch blank paper. While students worked on their sketches, I went around the room to work one-on-one with those who had problems with their graphing calculators. I had students label their graphs with the letter on the envelope that their data came from. At that point, class was about to end, so I told the students we would study their graphs the next day.

Day 3

The next day, I posted a graph from each group (spread out) around the room and gave students copies of the survey questions without the corresponding letter labels. To begin I had each group go find its graph and stand in front of it. I instructed the groups to study each graph when they approached it to attempt to determine which survey question the data represented. I asked them to write the letter of the graph next to the survey question they believed it belonged with once they had decided which graph went with which question. I gave them three to four minutes at each graph and then instructed them to move clockwise around the room. This enabled the groups to remain spread out around the room. When the groups were finished, I sent them around the room one more time to give them a chance to check their answers. Some wanted to change their answers after they saw later graphs. I gave them one to two minutes at each graph and then asked them to return to their seats. One by one, we went around the room and students told me what their guesses were for each of the plots. I wrote the survey question numbers that were given by the students for each plot on the graph paper. Then I revealed the actual answers. We discussed several things about each graph.

1. What information helped you match the plot with the question?

2. What made it difficult for you to match the plot with the question?

3. Where there any data points that seemed unreasonable?

This activity enabled students to think critically about their choices when matching the graphs and the questions. In addition, it encouraged dialogue among the students. Some questions were easier to match with a graph than others. For example, students were able to identify the graph for age because there was a limited range of numbers, mainly the numbers 12 and 13. Similarly, the graph for the number of minutes of TV in a week was an easier graph to identify because it had a larger range of numbers than the other questions would obtain. The hardest graphs to match with a question were the number of books read and the number of times the student had moved (questions 3 and 6). Both had similar data, and there were zeroes and data points in the teens in both cases. This was done intentionally. While the possible questions to pose are numerous, consideration must be given to the resulting data.

Question 3 provided a nice introduction to *outliers*. Although we did not formally discuss outliers at this time, I did refer to them to introduce the new vocabulary in context. Due to the informal, non-threatening introduction of the concept of box-and-whisker plots, the use of technology, the opportunity to work in collaborative groups, and the opportunity for active participation, students learned how to develop and interpret box-and-whisker plots.

What's Faster Than a Speeding Cheetah?

In *What's Faster Than a Speeding Cheetah?*, Robert E. Wells (1997) begins by describing how fast an ostrich can travel. With each page, the animals and objects grow increasingly faster in speed until, finally, Wells describes the speed of light.

In this investigation, students use the rates given in the book to determine the time it would take each of the animals and objects to reach the same destination, the Moon.

MATERIALS

What's Faster Than a Speeding Cheetah? **worksheet,** 1 per student (see Blackline Masters)

Introducing the Investigation

I began the lesson by reading *What's Faster Than a Speeding Cheetah?* to the class. I did not, however, show the chart at the end of the book, which illustrates how long it would take each of the animals and objects mentioned in the book to get to the Moon. Instead, I assigned the students the task of figuring out the time it would take each animal and object to reach the Moon. Before I sent the students off to work on this problem, I asked them what they would need to know before they began.

"We need to know how many miles it is to the Moon," Emily stated.

"How could we find that out?" I asked.

"Look it up in an encyclopedia or search on the computer," John answered.

"Would you like to use my computer to find that out for us?" I asked John. He agreed.

"While John is doing that, what else do we need to know?" I asked.

"The speeds of each of the animals," Eddie responded.

"Where could we get that information?" I asked.

"From the book," Eddie said.

I gave each student a copy of the worksheet (see Blackline Masters). The chart listed the animals and objects and their speeds in one column, and the second column was left blank. I told them they were to record how long it would take for each animal or object to get to the Moon in the second column. I had the students look over the chart to be sure they understood what they were to do next.

By this time John had found that the average distance between Earth and the Moon is about 239,000 miles. I asked the students to record this on the top of their papers, organized them into groups of three, and had them begin working on the assignment. Many used calculators at this point to assist with the long division.

After about fifteen minutes, I asked the students to stop working and report on some of their initial findings. John explained that he found the time it would take the ostrich by taking 239,000 (distance to the Moon in miles) and dividing by 45 (speed of the ostrich in miles per hour); he got 5,311 hours. The others agreed.

For the other problems, most students had reported solutions in hours. In some cases, the answers were in the hundreds or thousands of hours. I asked them if a number of hours that large made sense to them. I asked, "Do you really know how long that would take? Can you consider other options for reporting your answers?"

"We could change the hours into days," Margaret replied.

"And if we needed to, we could change it into months or even years," added Julie.

For most animals and objects, the students changed the hours into days by dividing by twenty-four. For the rocket ship and the meteoroid, they realized that a solution in hours was most reasonable. Finally, when they got to the speed of light, they realized a solution given in seconds made the most sense. The students were amazed at how fast light travels.

A Class Discussion

I said to the class, "Let's talk about the amount of time it would take for each of the animals and objects to reach the Moon. And, let's talk about whether your answers seem reasonable." I began the discussion by asking the students how long it would take an ostrich to get to the Moon.

"I got five thousand three hundred eleven hours. That didn't make a lot of sense to me, so I changed it to days and got about two hundred twenty-one days. It seems like a really long time, but an ostrich isn't very fast compared with a rocket ship," Mario commented.

"So you compared your answers with the rocket ship?" I asked.

"Yes, at least for most of them we did that," Mario responded.

"We compared all of our answers with each other. As we went through the book, the animals or objects got faster and faster, so we expected them to take less and less time to get to the Moon," Yvonne reasoned.

"That's an interesting observation," I responded.

"We had the supersonic jet taking longer to reach the Moon than the falcon, but then we realized we were wrong. We thought about it like Yvonne said and we went back and fixed it," Alan said.

"I don't know if I agree with the rocket. In technology class, we learned that a rocket does not move at the same rate throughout its journey to the Moon. It goes at different speeds," Doug shared.

"Yes, and I don't think that the ostrich, the cheetah, and the falcon could run or fly all that way to the Moon without stopping to rest or something and probably would not be able to keep up that pace for an extended period of time. I think it would take longer than we really calculated for them to get to the Moon," Sue argued.

Soon students questioned the plane and jet solutions. Jason asked, "Wouldn't they have to stop for gas?"

Doug also informed me that planes and jets weren't built for space travel and probably wouldn't make it all the way to the moon. The students began discussing the animals again and wondered about their oxygen—how could we expect them to get to the Moon without an oxygen supply? Clearly, these students took the idea of a "reasonable answer" seriously!

A Writing Assignment

I asked the students to write an explanation for how they calculated the time it took for one of the animals or objects on the chart to reach the Moon, being as specific as possible. Many students wrote more than one draft to explain their thinking. After everyone had completed a draft, I paired up the students and asked that each

Using the speed of each animal or object below, figure out how much time it would take that animal or object to get to the Moon.

At this speed . . .	It would take . . . to get to the Moon.
Ostrich (45 miles per hour)	5311 hours ≅ 221 days
Cheetah (70 miles per hour)	3414 hours ≅ 142 days
Peregrine Falcon (200 miles per hour)	1195 hours ≈ 49 days
Propeller Plane (300 miles per hour)	796 hour ≅ 33 days
Supersonic Jet (1,400 miles per hour)	170 hours ≅ 7 days
Rocket Ship (25,000 miles per hour)	9.5 hours
Meteoroid (150,000 miles per hour)	1.5 hours
Light (186,000 miles per second)	1.2 seconds

Explain how you found the answer to *one* of the above problems.

I found the answer to the rocket ship question by taking 239,000 miles (witch is how many miles it is to the moon), divided by 25,000, (wich is how fast the rocket ship gose per hour), and got 9.5 hours, (wich is how long it would take the rocket ship to get to the moon). I did not divide this by 24, (the number of hours in a day) becaus there is less than 24 hours near

student help his or her partner write the clearest, most detailed explanation possible. I encouraged them to question their partners as to why they were doing what they were doing. The biggest change that students made to their work was to explain a reason for the calculations they were making.

The students worked hard to describe what they did and from where they derived the numbers they were using. (See Figures 14–1 and 14–2.) They came away from the investigation with a much better understanding of rate.

Using the speed of each animal or object below, figure out how much time it would take that animal or object to get to the Moon.

At this speed . . .	It would take . . . to get to the Moon.
Ostrich (45 miles per hour)	5,311 hours ≈ 221 days ≈ 7.3 months
Cheetah (70 miles per hour)	3414 hours ≈ 142 days ≈ 4.6 months
Peregrine Falcon (200 miles per hour)	1195 hours ≈ 49 days ≈ 1.6 months
Propeller Plane (300 miles per hour)	796 hours ≈ 33 days ≈ 1.1 months
Supersonic Jet (1,400 miles per hour)	170 hours ≈ 7 days ≈ 0.2 months
Rocket Ship (25,000 miles per hour)	9.5 hours ≈ 0.3 days ≈ 0.01 months
Meteoroid (150,000 miles per hour)	1.5 hours ≈ 0.06 days ≈ 0.002
Light (186,000 miles per second)	1.2 seconds

Explain how you found the answer to *one* of the above problems.

We took 239,000 miles divided by 4.5 miles to find how many hours it would take (5,311) an ostrich to get to the moon. Then we took 5,311 hours divided that by 24 to find how many days it would take (221) to the moon. Final I would take 221 and divide that by 30 because there's an average of 30 days in a month.

Part Two

Additional Ideas

Animal Farm

George Orwell's American classic, *Animal Farm* (1946), is a satire of the Russian Revolution. Animals, discontent with man's leadership on the farm, chase the owner away and begin to run the farm themselves with basic commandments of equitable behavior. Over time, the pigs begin to play more and more of a dictatorial role until they become much like the humans that had run the farm. As time goes on, the animals feel that they are receiving less food, but Squealer states that "every class of food-stuff had increased by 200 per cent, 300 per cent, or 500 per cent, as the case might be" (early in Chapter 8). This book is commonly a required text in middle school.

This investigation can be used when students are reading this book in their language arts class. The focus of this lesson is on percent increase. Percent increase measures the *change* from the original amount. Students often confuse 200 per cent of the original with 200 per cent increase. For example, 200 per cent of the horses' ration (8 cups of oats) is 16 cups; however, a 200 per cent *increase* would mean an increase of 16, for a total of 24 cups. Here an effective strategy is presented for helping students differentiate between the two and make sense of percent increase.

MATERIALS

paper strips

Introducing the Investigation

In this investigation, students will explore percent increase of various food rations. Give students the following original rations for the farm animals:

Food Ration List

    Horse: 8 cups of oats   Hen: 0.75 cups of corn
    Cow: 2 gallons of grain   Sheep: 4 quarts of grain

Using the horse rations as an example, share with students the following two ways to illustrate percent using paper strips. First, students can make a single strip, fold it in equal-length sections, and label it with percents. See the partial strip below for the horse rations:

Students may shade the original amount (100 percent) as a reminder of the original amount. Another strategy is to have strips for each 100 percent. So, for a problem using 200 percent increase, a student would have the original strip plus two additional strips of equal size. Using one of the two strategies, have students determine the rations for each animal if its food ration is increased by 200 percent, 300 percent, and 500 percent. Students may use mental math, paper and pencil, or calculators to calculate these rations. Allow students to share how they solved the different percents for the different animals. You can extend this activity by using more difficult percent increases, such as 50 percent and 175 percent.

A Follow-up Problem

While finding the new amount when given the percent increase is challenging, it is even more difficult for students to find the percent increase when given the old ration and the new ration. As a second investigation, give students before and after amounts and have them find the percent increase. For example, the horse feed goes from 6 cups of oats to 12 cups of oats (100 percent increase), or the sheep's hay goes from 4 pounds to 10 pounds (150 percent increase). Ask students to share their strategies for solving these problems and how these problems compare with the first type of problems that they did. Finally, ask students to explain what the difference is between percent of a number and percent increase.

Anno's Hat Tricks

Anno's Hat Tricks, by Akihiro Nozaki (1985), is a logical reasoning book featuring three characters—Tom, Hannah, and Shadowchild (the reader). Throughout the book, the author poses different situations regarding what color hat each character is wearing (red or white). In one situation, for example, there are two red hats and one white hat available; Tom is wearing a red hat. The author asks Shadowchild if he or she knows whether his or her hat is red or white. Shadowchild does not know. But, *after* Tom says his own hat is definitely red, Shadowchild can deduct that his or her hat must be white (that is the only way Tom would know that his hat was red).

The logic becomes more challenging as the book progresses. The appendix explains some strategies for determining who is wearing what color hat (including tree diagrams) and describes how to extend the problems. This investigation calls on students' deductive reasoning while it engages them in finding the probability of simple and conditional events.

MATERIALS

Anno's Hat Tricks statement cards that say "I don't know," "My hat is red," and "My hat is white," 1 set per student (see Blackline Masters)

Anno's Hat Tricks color card deck that has three cards saying "red" and two cards saying "white," 1 deck per group of three (see Blackline Masters)

Introducing the Investigation

Before you read *Anno's Hat Tricks* aloud, distribute a set of statement cards (see Blackline Masters) to each student. Tell the students that, while you read the story, they should imagine they are the character Shadowchild. When you get to the questions in the book that ask Shadowchild which color hat he or she is wearing, have each student pick the card he or she thinks is right and hold it up. The narrator of the story will soon confirm the correct answer. Continue through the scenarios, allowing students time to reason about what color Shadowchild's hat is. For the last situation, have students each write a rationale for what color hat Shadowchild is wearing.

Next, place students in groups of three to explore new logic problems using the color card decks (see Blackline Masters). Explain to students that there are three "red" cards and two "white" cards, just like the story. With cards facedown, each student in a group draws a card and holds it facing out so that he or she cannot see it, but the two others can. Each student is to guess what color card he or she has. Students take turns, announcing "I don't know," "My card is red," or "My card is white." After each student has had a turn, each makes his or her final decision about his or her card color and explains how he or she knows (or why he or she can't tell).

Additional Problems

To explore probability, ask students to figure out the probability that Shadowchild's hat is red in the different hat scenarios in the book (e.g., two reds and one white). Have students refigure the probability that Shadowchild is wearing red *after* seeing what color Tom is wearing (conditional probability). As a class, create a tree diagram to illustrate the possibilities for Tom and Shadowchild (two red and one white hats). Discuss how the tree can be used to find probabilities and conditional probabilities the students have just found. In groups, have students create a new tree diagram for Tom, Hannah, and Shadowchild (three red and two white hats). (See Figure 16–1.)

Students can solve various probability questions such as the following:

P (Tom and Shadowchild have red hats)
P (all three have red hats)
P (at least two have red hats)
P (no one has a red hat)
P (one person is wearing red)
P (only Hannah is wearing red)
P (Tom and Hannah have different-colored hats)
P (at least one person is wearing red)

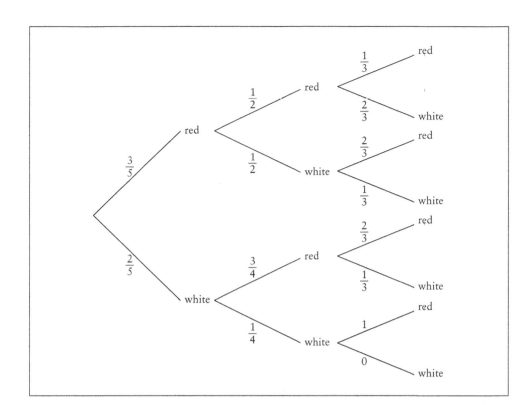

Figure 16–1: A tree diagram illustrating the conditional probability of selecting a red or white hat.

After students have solved these problems, they can share their answers and the strategies they used to solve them. Some may use the tree diagram; some may create a list of all the possible combinations. These two approaches can be compared to see how the tree diagram shows all the different possibilities.

Factastic Book of 1,001 Lists

As the title implies, Russell Ash's *Factastic Book of 1,001 Lists* (1999) is full of lists. There are lists related to sports, authors, geography, science, amazing people, industry, deadly snakes, countries with the most Internet users, and so on. In addition to having lists read to them, students enjoy reading this book on their own as time allows. Because the book is full of data, it is a perfect prompt for students to create graphs and analyze data.

The first investigation in this lesson explores box-and-whisker plots and bar graphs, asking students to create the graphs and explain the advantages of each. The second investigation explores creating a circle graph. The type of graph created depends on the type of data. For example, box-and-whisker plots require numerical data and are used to illustrate the spread of data. A circle graph can use nonnumerical data, but the data must add up to 100 percent. In addition to creating appropriate graphs from the lists, students collect local data to see how it compares with the lists in the book.

MATERIALS

Investigation 1
optional: transparency of list being used

Investigation 2
optional: 2-foot strips of adding machine tape, 1 per student
optional: transparency of list being used

Investigation 1: Box-and-Whisker Plot

Share several interesting lists from *Factastic Book of 1,001 Lists* to read to the students. Select one list that lends itself to creating a box-and-whisker plot. I selected "Top Albums of All Time," from the "Popular Music Artists" section, which listed the names of top albums and the estimated sales for each. I wanted students to use this information to create box-and-whisker plots.

Before reading the list, ask each student to write down his or her favorite album. Ask students what they think might be the most popular album of all time. Read the list to the students and then ask students if these top-selling albums are similar in their sales. What would be the median of the album sales? The mean? Project a transparency of the list (or write it on the blackboard) and ask students to each create a box-and-whisker plot for the data.

After they have finished, ask them to also calculate the mean with their calculators. *Thriller* by Michael Jackson is an outlier on this list. Discuss with students the impact an outlier has on the median and the mean. Ask students to each create a bar graph of the data and to be ready to discuss the advantages of each type of graph. Ask students what other graph types are appropriate for this data and which ones would be inappropriate. Students should recognize that a histogram is inappropriate, for example, because the data isn't in intervals; if they use a circle graph, they are finding the percent of the sales among the best-sellers *only* and not of all albums.

Investigation 2: Circle Graph

The list I selected for the second investigation was the cruise ship shopping list, because it was appropriate for creating a circle graph. The list gives the amount spent on various foods and drinks for a fourteen-day cruise. Project a transparency of the list (or write it on the board) and ask students to figure out the purchased food per day and create circle graphs illustrating what percent is spent on each type of food excluding the beverages (e.g., fruits, meat, potatoes, and so on). There are several strategies that can be used for creating a circle graph. The formal way is to figure out the percent each item represents, convert that to the number of degrees out of 360, and create a sector that size with a protractor. An alternative approach is to use strips of paper (adding machine tape works well) that are shaded and then wrapped into a circle and taped. Give each student a strip about 2 feet long and have them fold it into ten equal sections (to represent 10 percent each). Students calculate the percent each item is of the total. They may do additional folding as needed to get the sectors to the correct size. Each food is shaded in a different color and labeled with the appropriate name. Once the strip is labeled, it is wrapped into a circle, taped, and set on a piece of paper. Then, students can find the center of the circle and draw radii to create the sectors.

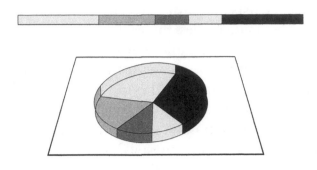

Additional Problems

Students can also collect their own data and compare it with the lists' data in the book. "Highest-Grossing Films of All Time," for example, is a good list for this investigation. Read the list to the students. Then, ask students to create a bar graph (or a circle graph) of the data. After students have completed their graphs, ask them if *highest-grossing* means the same thing as *most popular* (students may note that movies have gotten more expensive, there are more people, and more movie theaters). Even though these factors are true, these movies are considered the most popular. Ask students how this list would compare to the most popular films now. Place students in groups of two or three and ask them to discuss how they would design a survey on the most popular films and how they would collect data. Ask them to consider who they would want to survey and how many people they should survey. After they have had a few minutes to discuss how they will complete their surveys, have groups share their ideas. Then ask students to collect their data. If they are collecting data beyond the students in the class, you will need to give them sufficient time to collect them. Once each group has collected its data, ask students to create another bar graph (or circle graph) and compare the results. As an alternative, the class can compile all student data first and then create bar graphs with all the data and compare the book's data to the students'.

Far North

Will Hobbs's *Far North* (1996) takes place deep in the wilderness of the Northwest Territories. Gabe, the main character, is a passenger on a small floatplane that lands on a lake to look at a waterfall. When the engine won't start again, Gabe and Raymond, his roommate from boarding school and the other passenger on the plane, scramble to get off the plane. The pilot and the plane soon take a deadly plunge over the falls. This leaves the passengers stranded in the wilderness of the Northwest Territories with winter quickly approaching.

In this investigation, students analyze several land areas, create scale drawings to represent these areas, and interpret the corresponding population density for each of the land areas. The investigation requires students to do some research about the land areas and populations of the Northwest Territories, Alaska, and their own state.

MATERIALS

centimeter-squared paper, 1 per student
(see Blackline Masters)

atlas or computer with Internet access (to
retrieve data on state areas and populations)

Introducing the Investigation

Read aloud Chapter 1 of *Far North*. Go back to the part of the chapter where Clint is telling Gabe what he should know about the Northwest Territories. He says, "It stretches from the Yukon practically to within spitting distance of Greenland. The N.W.T is twice as big as Alaska." To begin exploring how big these places are, students will need to conduct research to find the land area of Alaska. (There are 570,374 square miles of land in Alaska.) Ask students to look up the area of their state. Using the data from their state, Alaska, and the NWT, have students develop comparison statements, such as "Alaska is about twelve times the size of my state," or "Colorado is about one-fifth the size of Alaska."

Distribute a sheet of centimeter-squared paper to each student and ask that each sketch a scale model of the land area of the NWT, Alaska, and your state. These areas should be drawn so that the area of Alaska is within the area of the NWT and the area of your state is within Alaska. This will help them conceptualize the size of the Northwest Territories by linking it back to something they are familiar with.

Two paragraphs later in Chapter 1, Clint says, "Only sixty thousand people live in the entire N.W.T, and almost a third of them live in the city of Yellowknife." Read this statement to the students and ask them to find the population of their own state, given in the most recent census. Have them also find the population of Alaska and the NWT given in the most recent census (they can look this up or you can tell them). Ask students what they think the term *population density* means. If students don't understand the phrase, explain to them that it is the average number of people per square mile. Allow students time to find the population densities for each of the three locations—NWT, Alaska, and their own state. Ask students to find a state that would have a population density most closely resembling that of the NWT. Finally, ask students to describe the challenges and benefits of living in places with very high and very low population densities.

The 512 Ants on Sullivan Street

In Carol Losi's *The 512 Ants on Sullivan Street* (1997), a young girl and her caretaker go to a picnic. In rhyming verse, we hear that 1 ant carries away a crumb, then 2 ants carry away a piece of plum, followed by 4 ants taking a barbecued chip. Each time new ants arrive, there are twice as many as the time before and they take a different kind of food. In the end, 512 ants take away the dessert.

This activity involves students in creating tables, graphs, and equations for doubling patterns. A doubling pattern is represented symbolically as 2^n, which is a very different pattern than $2n$, though students often confuse the two. Tables and graphs can help distinguish the uniqueness of the doubling pattern.

MATERIALS

centimeter-squared paper (see Blackline Masters)

optional: graphing calculators or computers with spreadsheet programs

Introducing the Investigation

Read *The 512 Ants on Sullivan Street* to the class. Provide calculators for students to use for exploring patterns in the numbers. Ask students to describe what patterns they notice in the ants' arrival to take away the food. As a class, create a table on the board, recording in Column 1 the number of trips and in Column 2 the number of ants. Record the data from the book (up to 512 ants). Ask students if they can predict what the next number of ants would be. Organize students in pairs and challenge them to (1) predict the tenth, twentieth, and thirtieth trip to the picnic and (2) determine a rule, in words and in symbols, that would work for any number of trips to the picnic.

As a way to emphasize the difference between 2^n and $2n$, ask students to consider a different ant pattern: the first to show up is 2 ants, then 4 ants, then 6 ants (not 8), and so on. Ask students to develop a table for this pattern and describe the rule in words and in symbols for the nth trip to the picnic.

Ask students to use their tables and centimeter-squared paper, graphing calculators, or a spreadsheet program (e.g., Excel) to create graphs of the two ant patterns described previously. Have pairs refer to their tables, explanations of each rule, symbolic representations of each rule, and graphs to discuss and record ways in which these two patterns are different and the same. Pairs can share their comparisons with the whole class.

(**Note:** This book can also be used as an extension to the activity described for *One Hundred Hungry Ants*. Students can use the number of ants going to this picnic and determine the different arrays for each trip. For example, on the sixth trip, sixty-four ants went to the picnic, so students can find the possible arrays for sixty-four marching ants.)

Holes

Louis Sachar's *Holes* (1998), a clever and popular middle school novel, begins with Stanley Yelnats going to Camp Green Lake, a correctional facility for boys. The camp is located in the middle of a desert. Every day, each boy has to dig one hole that is "five feet deep and five feet across in any direction." They use their 5-foot shovels to measure the diameter and depth of each cylindrical hole. The bully of the group, X-Ray, always claims the same shovel, which he says is "a fraction of an inch" shorter than the others. Day after day, the boys dig holes. Stanley begins to notice strange things about the people running the camp and eventually uncovers the reason for digging the holes.

This book provides a wonderful opportunity to explore the volume of cylinders. Just as the area of a circle increases significantly with a small change in diameter, the volume of a cylinder also changes dramatically. To do this investigation, students need to know or have access to the formulas for area of a circle and volume of a cylinder. Students also compare the dirt removed by the boys for multiple holes. As they determine the dirt removed after one week, two weeks, and so on, they can see that the difference of dirt removed between X-Ray's holes and the other boys' holes is significant over time.

MATERIALS

centimeter-squared paper, 2 per student
  (see Blackline Masters)

compass, 1 per student

ruler, 1 per student

Introducing the Investigation

Read Chapters 1 and 2 of *Holes* to the class. Also read the beginning of Chapter 7, where the author discusses the shovels that the boys choose. Ask students if they think X-Ray would be removing much less dirt than Stanley if his shovel was $\frac{1}{2}$ inch shorter. Then, as an initial investigation, ask students to use a compass and a ruler, if necessary, to draw two circles to scale, such that one is 5 inches in diameter and one is 4.5 inches in diameter. Ask students to find and compare the areas of the two circles.

To explore the difference in volume of the holes in the story, first have students work in pairs to estimate the difference in the volume of dirt that would be removed from the two holes (in cubic feet). After students have made their predictions, distribute calculators and ask them to determine the volume of dirt removed for Stanley's hole, which has a diameter and depth of 5 feet (approximately 169,560 cubic inches or 98.13 cubic feet, using 3.14 for pi). Ask students to do the same for X-Ray's hole, which has a diameter and depth of 4 feet 11.5 inches (approximately 165,356.22 cubic inches or 95.69 cubic feet, using 3.14 for pi).

One of the challenges in this task is selecting units. Students must decide whether to convert to feet at the beginning, or to start with inches and convert to cubic feet at the end. Students who select to use inches might try dividing by 12, but 1728 cubic inches are in one cubic foot ($12 \times 12 \times 12$). Students who select to convert to feet prior to computing the volume will need to determine the appropriate decimal for 4 feet, 11.5 inches (4.96 feet).

Once students find the difference in the volumes of each hole, have them create a context for illustrating how much less dirt X-Ray had to remove (4,203.78 cubic inches or 2.44 cubic feet). For example, students might use a container in the room and determine how many times it would be filled with dirt. Another option is for students to determine the dimensions of a box that would hold all the extra dirt that Stanley had to dig each day.

In order to further investigate the difference in dirt removal over time, students can determine the amount of dirt removed after one week, two weeks, or after six months (the time Stanley is at Camp Green Lake). After six months the difference is approximately 444 cubic feet (or 16 cubic yards)!

The King's Giraffe

The King's Giraffe, by Mary Jo Collier and Peter Collier (1996), is a true story of the pasha (ruler) of Egypt giving the gift of a giraffe to the king of France. In 1826, the giraffe sails to Marseilles. When she arrives, there is no way for her to get to Paris except to walk. With beautiful illustrations, the book describes the travels of the giraffe who arrives in Paris in 1827.

In this lesson, students will estimate time and distance. Because the numbers are fairly large, students have the opportunity to develop number sense for large numbers. Also, students will study rate, including how it is represented in a table and in a graph. Rate is an important middle school topic, leading to the development of slope.

MATERIALS

map of the Mediterranean region, including France and Egypt

centimeter–squared paper, 1 sheet per group (see Blackline Masters)

Introducing the Investigation

Prior to reading *The King's Giraffe* to students, ask them (using the map as a reference) how long they think it would take to travel by boat across the Mediterranean Sea from Egypt to France and then to walk through France to Paris. You may want to record estimates on the board or have students record estimates on their own. Next, read the story to the class. Ask students to determine the rate at which the giraffe walked through France (they can do a daily rate and/or an hourly rate). You may ask the students what information in the story they would like to revisit in order to solve the problem (data is also provided in the back of the book). With students working in pairs or small groups, have them prepare a report of the time it took to walk from Marseilles to Paris (six weeks to go 425 miles), using calculators if they prefer. They will have to make decisions about how many hours the travelers walked each day. They will also have to assume a constant rate over the six weeks. Group reports should include a written description of how they set up the problem and an explanation of the rate of travel per hour, a table illustrating how much land was covered for each hour of travel, and a graph of the data from the table. Students should be able to explain how rate can be found in the table and in the graph. Since students may not have a sense for the distance between Marseilles and Paris, you may have them find a similar comparison that would be more familiar. For example, if they were to leave their hometown and walk 425 miles, where could they end up?

The Missing Piece

The Missing Piece, by Shel Silverstein (1976), is about a circle that has lost a piece (a sector). He looks all over for his missing piece, only to find pieces that are the wrong size. After many trials, he finds his missing piece. This is a very short book and can be read in a couple of minutes.

In the investigation, students will determine the central angle of a sector of a circle, the length of an arc, and the percent the sector and the arc are of the circle. To do this, students can use string to find the percent the missing arc is of the entire circle and generate the other answers from this information. They can also begin with measuring the central angle and then find the other answers from this information. Students will need to know the formulas for finding the area and the circumference of a circle.

MATERIALS

paper circles, each with a different-sized sector missing (Possible missing pieces could have the following sectors missing: 18° [5%], 36° [10%], 45° [12.5%], 54° [15%], 72° [20%]. Any central angles less than 90° work nicely with this book. Paper plates can be used to make the circles.)

string, 1 piece per pair of students, at least the length of the circumference of the circles

protractors, 1 per pair of students

rulers, 1 per pair of students

Introducing the Investigation

Read *The Missing Piece* to the class. Introduce the activity by showing a paper circle with a missing piece that has a central angle of 45 degrees ($\frac{1}{8}$ or 12.5 percent of the circle missing). Ask students to estimate the central angle and the percent of the circle that is missing. This will allow students to begin thinking about the difference between the total degrees of a circle (360) and the total percent of a circle (100). Then give each pair of students a circle with a missing piece, as well as a protractor, a ruler, and a piece of string. Save the "missing pieces," each labeled with the central angle and/or the percent of the circle it represents, for later. Ask each pair to help the circle find its missing piece by figuring—in any order the two choose— (1) the interior angle of the missing piece, (2) the area of the circle that is missing and the percent of the missing circle it represents, and (3) the length of the missing arc and the percent it represents of the whole circumference. Have students describe their missing piece and claim it from the collection of missing pieces.

Using a large table (use chart paper or the blackboard), have each pair record its information so that the data from all the circles are shown on the table. Have students share what is alike and different about the circles. As a follow-up or an assessment, ask students to answer the following questions, explaining why or why not: Will the area of the sector change if the circle gets bigger? (Yes.) Will the arc length change? (Yes.) Will the central angle change? (No.) Will the percent the missing piece represents of the whole circle change? (No.) Allow students time to build larger or smaller circles to test their hypotheses.

My Little Sister Ate One Hare

In Bill Grossman's counting book, *My Little Sister Ate One Hare* (1996), a brother tells the story of his sister's diet. First, she eats one hare; next she eats two snakes, then three ants, and so on. Her eating pattern continues until she eats ten peas, which makes her throw up all the things she has already eaten. The context of this counting book makes it ideal for middle school students.

In this probability investigation, students complete an experiment with selecting food items (on cards) to see how often they select each kind of food. In the experiment, students look at a small number of trials (fifty-five) and a large number (class totals). After the experiment, students determine the theoretical probability, or what would be the expected number of outcomes, for each type of food. An important idea in this investigation is that as the number of trials increases, the experiment is more likely to resemble the theoretical probability.

MATERIALS

brown paper bags or other containers, 1 per pair of students

My Little Sister Ate One Hare food cards (1 hare, 2 snakes, etc.), 1 deck per pair of students (see Blackline Masters)

My Little Sister Ate One Hare record table, 1 per student (see Blackline Masters)

Introducing the Investigation

Read *My Little Sister Ate One Hare* to the class. Then ask the class to estimate and then figure out how many items were eaten (1 hare + 2 snakes + 3 ants ... + 10 peas, for a total of 55 items). Pose the following situation to students: *All these items are scattered about the room and the sister, in cleaning up, is going to reach down and grab one item off the floor. What are the chances she will get a shrew? A worm?*

Have students work in pairs to complete an experiment. Each pair needs a deck of food cards (see Blackline Masters) and a paper bag or other container. Have them place the cards in the bag and shake it up. Explain that they are going to draw and replace the cards fifty-five times and record their data in the *My Little Sister Ate One Hare* table (see Blackline Masters). After completing the experiment, have students complete columns two through four on the Blackline Master using a calculator to determine percent.

On the board, create a table for recording the class data, with a row for each pair to record its totals. (See Figure 23–1.)

After students have completed the experiment, have them record their data on the class table (the number of times each item occurred, not the percentage). As groups are recording their data, they should begin to determine the theoretical probabilities of selecting each of the items, recording each expected value as a percent under the last

Figure 23–1: Class data is collected on this table so that students can compare the results of their own smaller experiment with the larger set of data collected by all groups combined.

	Hares	Snakes	Ants	Shrews	Bats	Mice	Polliwogs	Worms	Lizards	Peas
Group 1										
Group 2										
Group 3										
. .										
Total										
Fraction										
Percent										
Theoretical Probability										

column in their own tables. The theoretical probability is based on the logical analysis of the problem, assuming that all events are equally likely. For example, five of the fifty-five items are bats, so $\frac{5}{55}$ or $\frac{1}{11}$ or 9 percent of the draws *should* be bats. In an experiment with a small number of trials, the experiment can differ significantly from the theoretical, but as the number of trials increases the experimental results resemble the theoretical probability more closely.

Ask groups to study their own data and the class data and compare those to the theoretical probabilities. Ask each student to write (1) his or her rationale for why the experiment might differ from the theoretical and (2) whether it matters how many trials one has in a probability experiment and why.

A Follow-up Problem

As an alternative or an extension, students can do similar experiments related to groupings of food items, for example, the probability of selecting four-legged animals.

One Hundred Hungry Ants

In *One Hundred Hungry Ants*, by Elinor J. Pinczes (1993), the ants are marching toward a picnic and trying to figure out the marching formation that will get them there the quickest. Initially they are marching in a single-file line of one hundred, then two lines of fifty, then four lines of twenty-five, and so on.

In this lesson, arrays and rectangles are used to develop the concept of factors. While rectangles are quadrilaterals with opposite sides congruent and parallel, and all 90-degree angles, arrays are rectangular arrangements of equal rows of discrete items, such as ants, chairs in a theatre, or trees in an orchard. With rectangles, the lengths of the sides can be considered factors and the area of the rectangle the product; with arrays, the numbers of objects in each row and column are factors and the total number of objects in the array is the product. Exploring arrays and rectangles helps students learn about prime, composite, and square numbers. The lesson also introduces the idea that square numbers, such as 16, have an odd number of factors because one of the factor pairs (for example, 4×4 for the number 16) uses the same factor twice. All non-square natural numbers have an even number of factors.

MATERIALS

dot paper (see Blackline Masters)

30 pieces of large construction paper or newsprint

optional: number cards from 1 to 30

optional: color tiles or counters

Introducing the Investigation

Read *One Hundred Hungry Ants* aloud. Each time the ants rearrange themselves, ask students to predict what the next arrangement might be. After reading the story, list the different ant formations on the board:

$$1 \times 100$$
$$2 \times 50$$
$$4 \times 25$$
$$5 \times 20$$
$$10 \times 10$$

Ask different students to represent each array on dot paper (see Blackline Masters). Ask the students to identify other possible ant arrangements, such as 20×5 and 25×4. List these on the board:

$$20 \times 5$$
$$25 \times 4$$
$$50 \times 2$$
$$100 \times 1$$

Talk about how twenty lines of five, for example, would be a different formation from the five lines of twenty in the story. Also talk with students about how the numbers in each of the arrays can be rearranged to form another array; that is, if four rows of twenty-five is possible, then twenty-five rows of four is also possible. This is because four and twenty-five are a factor pair for one hundred. Have the students identify all of the factors of one hundred.

Have students work in pairs to explore the factors of all the numbers from one to thirty. Pose the question: "What if there were a different number of ants? Could we figure out how many formations would be possible?" Assign two to three numbers to each pair and ask the students to create all the arrays possible for each one on dot paper. Either distribute cards with the numbers from *1* to *30* on them, or list the numbers from *1* to *30* on the board and write students' names next to them. You may want to make color tiles or counters available for students to use to build the arrays. Ask each pair to cut out all the possible arrays for its number, label the dimensions of the array, and tape or glue them to one large piece of paper labeled with that number of ants. Post the displays in order from one to thirty.

A Class Discussion

As a class, examine the arrays posted and look for patterns that occur across the numbers. Use the following questions for discussion, and incorporate appropriate vocabulary.

- Which numbers can be formed in exactly two ways—for example, seventeen rows of one and one row of seventeen? (These are *prime* numbers; all others except one are *composite*.)

- Which numbers have more than two possible arrays? (These are *composite* numbers.)

- Which numbers can be built in only one way? (Only the number one can be built in only one way; it is not prime or a composite.)

- Which numbers have arrays that are also squares? (These are *square* numbers. These numbers have an odd number of factors.)

- Which numbers have an even number of arrays? (These are non-square composite numbers.)

The Phantom Tollbooth

Milo, the main character in Norton Juster's *The Phantom Tollbooth* (1961/1989), is a bored young boy. When he arrives home from school one day, he is surprised to find a large box with a tollbooth in it. Driving through it, he finds himself in another world full of peculiar people and places. At one point, for example, Milo finds himself in Doldrums, where it is "unlawful, illegal, and unethical to think, think of thinking, surmise, presume, reason, meditate, or speculate."

The novel is full of puns and mathematical references and contains many options for launching mathematical investigations. Here are just two ideas—the first involves making circle graphs and the second is a permutation activity.

MATERIALS

Investigation 1
protractors, 1 per student
calculators, 1 per student

Investigation 2
none

Investigation 1: The Lethargarians's Schedule

In Chapter 2 of *The Phantom Tollbooth*, the Lethargarians describe their schedule (8:00 to 9:00 daydreaming, 9:00 to 9:30 nap, and so on). Read Chapters 1 and 2 to the class. Ask students questions about how they spend their day, such as How many hours do you spend in school? Sleeping? Studying? Eating? Doing recreation? Other activities? Have each student estimate about how much time he or she spends doing each of these activities. The time for all activities should add up to twenty-four hours. Have students create circle graphs of their estimated schedules.

Ask students to record throughout the next day the times they wake up, begin and end breakfast, ride in the car, and so on.

The following day, have students create circle graphs for their previous day, using their calculators to find the percentage of time they spent doing each type of activity. Ask students to compare their estimated schedules with the actual ones they collected. Also, ask students what surprised them about their schedules.

Investigation 2: Scrambled Words

Another place Milo visits is the Market Place, where aisles and aisles of words are for sale (see Chapter 4 and the beginning of Chapter 5). He visits with a Spelling Bee and meets a Humbug. The Humbug knocks over all the stalls in the Market Place, and all the words lie scrambled on the floor. This causes people to speak sentences that are out of order.

Read Chapter 4 and the beginning of Chapter 5 to the class. Have students each write down a three-word sentence, such as "Dogs eat bones." Ask them how many ways a three-word sentence could be said if the words were in any order (there are six ways). Have students share the ways and ask them to explain how they know they have all the ways. Students should have some organized way of listing the word combinations.

Organize students in small groups and have them repeat this process with four-word and five-word sentences. As students explore these word combinations, challenge them to search for any patterns that would lead to a shorter process for finding the number of possible combinations than writing all the word arrangements. Ask students to share the number of ways they could arrange a four-word sentence and a five-word sentence and to share any shortcuts or patterns they noticed. Have them apply their shortcuts to six-word sentences and see if they work. Students should notice the pattern that for a three-word sentence, they can multiply three times two to get the total number of combinations, and for a four-word sentence, they can multiply four times three times two. This can be written as a factoral (4!) and is used for finding permutations. Tree diagrams can be used to illustrate the permutations.

Roll of Thunder, Hear My Cry

Mildred D. Taylor's *Roll of Thunder, Hear My Cry* (1991) is the story of a young African American girl, Cassie, and her family living in Mississippi in the 1930s, during which time African Americans were threatened, ridiculed, and burned alive. Cassie experiences prejudice firsthand, but comes to know the determination of her family and their love of the land.

In this investigation, students are able to develop a more personal understanding of what life was like for those young African Americans attending school in the 1930s. They determine their own walking rates and create tables and graphs to represent how far they can travel in a given time. Students also use maps to identify starting and ending points for walks of certain distances as a way of developing a sense of distance.

MATERIALS

stopwatches or watches with second hands,
1 per group of three

map of your city, 1 per group of three

meter wheel

Note: You will also need access to a gymnasium, track, sidewalk, or other place where students can measure distance.

Introducing the Investigation

Read Chapter 1 of *Roll of Thunder, Hear My Cry* to the class. Ask students if they recall how long it took Cassie and her friends to get to school (it took one hour). Then ask them to share how they get to school and approximately how long it takes them. Ask them how far they think they could walk in one hour. Have each student record his or her individual estimate in kilometers (or miles) and then write a statement naming a beginning and an ending landmark for their walk, such as "I could walk from my house to the mall in an hour."

After the students record their estimates, ask them how they would determine the distance they could walk in an hour without actually walking for an hour. In groups of three, have students discuss strategies. Share strategies with the whole class.

You then may want each group to implement its own strategy, or you may opt to have everyone agree on one approach. Here is one way to collect the data: Students record how far they walk in thirty seconds. If distances are not marked off (like on a track), a meter wheel can be used to measure distances. Have students work in groups of three, assigning the following roles: timer, walker, and measurer. The timer will tell the walker when to start and stop, and the walker will walk normally for thirty seconds. At the completion of the walk, the measurer will measure the distance (in meters). The walker will record this information in his or her notebook. Roles rotate until each person has had his or her turn at each role.

Since distances in the United States are in miles (and this is more familiar to U.S. students) but school tracks and meter wheels are in metric distances, U.S. students will likely have to do conversions. They can either convert their estimates to kilometers, or convert their measured distances to miles. The formulas are as follows (k = kilometers, m = miles):

to convert miles to kilometers: $k = 0.62m$
to convert kilometers to miles: $m = 1.61k$

Using the data collected from his or her thirty-second walk and a calculator, each student determines the meters he or she could cover in an hour—in other words, the student's walking rate in meters per hour. Using their walking rates, students generate tables and graphs illustrating the distances they could travel in 1, 2, 3, or more hours. Recall that in the novel, Moe Turner, a friend of Cassie's, walked $3\frac{1}{2}$ hours to school. Ask the students how far they would go in that amount of time. How could they find this information on their tables? On their graphs? Often students don't have experience with distances. Therefore, once they have figured out how far they could go in 1 hour or in 3.5 hours, give each group a map of the city to study and ask each student to determine a beginning and ending place for a 1-hour walk and for a 3.5-hour walk.

The Tell-Tale Heart

The narrator in Edgar Allan Poe's short story "The Tell-Tale Heart" (1983) is driven mad by the "evil eye" of an old man. Every night at midnight, the narrator sneaks into the old man's room, slowly uncovers the lantern, but finds the old man's eye is closed. On the eighth night, when the light of the lantern falls on the old man's eye, the narrator finds it open and it drives him to kill the old man.

Poe describes at great length the beating of the old man's heart, both before and after his death. This becomes the launching point for making graphs of stories. Students make a graph of the volume of the beating heart over time.

MATERIALS

centimeter-squared paper, 1 sheet per student (see Blackline Masters)

Introducing the Investigation

Read aloud "The Tell-Tale Heart"; it will take about five to ten minutes. Then discuss the beating of the heart with the students. Ask students to describe in their own words the sound of the heartbeat throughout the story. The discussion should include conversation about the rate and the volume of a beating heart. Explain to the students that they are each going to make a graph illustrating how the volume of the beating heart changes over time. Pass out the centimeter-squared paper and have students label it with time on the x-axis and volume on the y-axis.

Next reread that part of the story where the narrator opens the lantern on the eighth night and finds the eye "wide, wide open." At this point, the narrator hears the sound of the old man's beating heart for the first time: "there came to my ears a low, dull, quick sound, such as a watch makes when enveloped in cotton." As you read, ask students to pay close attention to the amount of time that passes from the time the heartbeat starts to the time it stops. An estimate of the amount of time that passes is necessary for students to be able to number the x-axis (time) on their graphs. They will start the graph at zero minutes, which would be the moment the heartbeat started, and end the graph at their estimate of the last minute the heart was beating.

Continue rereading until the point where the old man dies and the heartbeat stops. Finish with the sentence "His eye would trouble me no more."

At this point ask students to work in small groups to determine how to number the graphs. They should use number of minutes for the variable time. They may want to create a scale for the volume, such as one they would find on the volume button of a stereo or radio. For example, they could use a scale of zero to ten, with zero

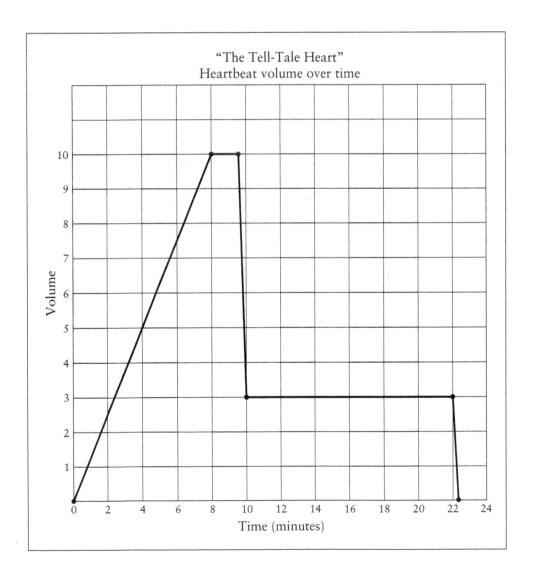

being no sound and ten being the loudest. Once the students have labeled their graphs, reread the part of the story about the heartbeat again. This time they will draw a line on the graph they created representing the change in volume over time as you read the passage.

When you have finished reading, ask students to compare their graphs and talk about any similarities or differences. What more would they need to know to make their graphs more accurate (for example, the exact time in minutes of phrases such as *every moment*, *at length*, and *some minutes*)? What would they change, if anything?

The Village of Round and Square Houses

In *The Village of Round and Square Houses*, Ann Grifalconi (1986) tells the story of a real village in a remote area of Cameroon, in which the men live in square houses and the women in round houses (the names of the houses refer to the floor shape inside each house). The book describes how the two different styles of houses came to be built.

In the lesson, students figure out whether the women's houses or the men's houses use less material, given that the area of the floor space is the same in both styles of home. The women's house (as illustrated in the book) has a cylinder for the walls and a cone for the roof. The men's house has a rectangular prism for the walls and a triangular prism for the roof. For students to determine the amount of material needed to build each house, they must determine the two-dimensional shapes that create the faces of the walls and the roof, find the area of each shape, and add the areas together. To do this investigation, students will need to know or have access to the surface area formulas for cones, cylinders, and prisms.

MATERIALS

centimeter-squared paper, 2–3 per person (see Blackline Masters)

optional: geometric solids, to show the shapes of the roof and bases of each house

Introducing the Investigation

After reading *The Village of Round and Square Houses*, ask the students which house style, the men's or the women's, they think would use less material to build. Ask students to select the geometric solid and identify the faces that represent the walls of women's house, the roof of the women's house, the walls of the men's house, and the roof of the men's house. After the students have shared their predictions, explain to them that they will be finding out how much material is needed to build each house in order to answer this question. On the board or an overhead transparency, write the following building guidelines:

The area of the floor space is 120 square feet for each house.
Walls must be 7 feet tall.
The height of each roof is 4 feet.
The bottom of the roof should be 1 foot wider than the walls on all sides (because of the overhang) (see below).

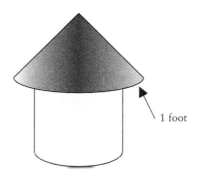

1 foot

Organize the students in pairs or small groups and ask them to find the surface areas of the walls and the roof for each house. Invite students to use the geometric solids to determine the shapes of all the surfaces. Students will need to keep in mind that, in the houses, not all faces of the related geometric shape actually require material. For example, for the cylindrical part of the women's house (the walls), there are no materials needed for the bases (assume no ceiling other than the roof). You may want to suggest that they first figure out the dimensions of the floor for each style of house and work from there. When students begin figuring the dimensions of the roofs, they will need to use some approximate values. After students have completed their computations, have them report how much material they found was needed for each style home.

Though it will vary from classroom to classroom, students likely will be able to figure out wall area and will need help with roof area. The following explains how to calculate both. You might have students figure out their own formulas for the walls and give them the formulas for the roofs.

Women's House

The area of the floor is 120 feet squared. Therefore the radius of the floor is 6.2 feet and the circumference of the room is 38.9 feet.

The walls are the sides of the cylinder, which when "unwrapped" makes a rectangle, with the length of the base being the circumference of the circle, and the height being the height of the walls (7 feet):

area of the walls (rounding to the nearest tenth):
38.9 × 7 = 272.3 square feet

The most challenging measurement to find is the area of the conic roof. Students will likely need to be provided with the formula below. The roof is a cone, with the radius of the base 1 foot more than the floor (radius of roof = 7.2 feet). The length of the diagonal from the tip of the roof to the bottom edge of the roof (p) can be found by using the Pythagorean theorem: $7.2^2 + 4^2 = p^2$ and in this case is 8.2 feet. The formula for the area of the roof is pi × r × p:

area of the roof: 3.14 × 7.2 × 8.2 = 185.4 square feet
total area for the women's house: 457.7 square feet

Men's House

The walls of the men's house are four rectangles, each one of them 11.0 feet by 7 feet.

area of the walls (rounding to the nearest tenth):
11.0 × 7 × 4 = 308 square feet

The roof is a triangular solid, but only two of the three rectangular sides require materials (see below).

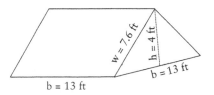

The material needed includes two rectangular sides and two triangular ends. The base of all sides of the roof has to be 2 feet longer than the walls (1 foot on every side), so all four sides have a base of 13.0 feet. The width (or height) of the rectangular sides is the hypotenuse of the triangle formed by the height and half the triangular base. The formula for surface area of the roof is the area of two triangles plus the area of two rectangles: $2 \times [\frac{1}{2}(b \times h)] + 2[b \times w]$.

area of the roof: $2[\frac{1}{2}(13.0 \times 4)] + 2[13.0 \times 7.6] =$
52 + 197.6 = 249.6 square feet
total area of the men's house: 557.6 square feet

What's Smaller Than a Pygmy Shrew?

Robert E. Wells begins *What's Smaller Than a Pygmy Shrew?* (1995) by comparing the size of a pygmy shrew with that of an elephant, then a ladybug, which is then compared with a water drop, a protozoa, and so on. Each page shows the previous item enlarged and the new item as a small piece of it; the book ends with electrons, protons, neutrons, and quarks.

Because this book focuses on very small items, it is an opportunity for students to develop their number sense about small numbers and decimal notation. First, students create scale drawings of bacteria in comparison with other items mentioned in the story (the dot of an *i* and a ladybug). Second, students shade decimal values to create a visual for comparing tenths, hundredths, thousandths, and ten thousandths.

MATERIALS

compass, 1 per student

construction paper or newsprint, 1 piece per group of four

millimeter-squared paper, several sheets per student (see Blackline Masters)

Introducing the Investigation

Before reading *What's Smaller Than a Pygmy Shrew?* to the class, ask students what they think is the smallest animal. Next ask what they think is the smallest living thing. Then read the story. Ask students what is bigger than bacteria and what is smaller than bacteria. On the page about bacteria, it says that thousands of bacteria could fit on the dot of an *i*. Assume that five thousand bacteria could fit on one dot. Therefore, a bacterium is $\frac{1}{5,000}$ of a dot, which is equivalent to $\frac{2}{10,000}$ or 0.0002.

Distribute the millimeter-squared paper (see Blackline Masters). Explain that students will be creating scale drawings to visualize comparisons from the book. Since a bacterium is too small to see, one millimeter square of the grid paper will represent one bacterium. Using this and the fact that a bacterium is 0.0002 of a dot, have students create an *i* that will have the bacterium (a square) as 0.0002 of its dot (a circle). Students will need calculators and compasses to do this. Give students time to explore and to select a strategy to make their circles. They might use the formula for the area of a circle and work backward to see what radius it would need, or they might use trial and error until they get a round shape with about 5,000 millimeter squares or 50 centimeter squares in it (the radius of the circle should be about 40 millimeters or 4 centimeters). After shading the dot on their millimeter paper, they will need to determine an appropriate size for the rest of the *i* and sketch it below the dot to complete the letter.

Next, in groups, have students create a ladybug relative in size to the dot of the *i* (ladybugs vary in size, but you can estimate the size to be about 8 millimeters in diameter, using a circle for the ladybug). Students can see how many dots it takes to form the radius of the ladybug. Students will determine that they can make about five dots, depending on the size of their dots. Therefore, in the scale drawing, using 40 millimeters for the radius of the dot of an *i* will likely result in a ladybug with a radius of about 200 millimeters (this can vary quite a lot, because students will likely draw different-sized dots). Sketching this will require taping sheets of the millimeter paper together. Once students have created the *i* and the ladybug, ask students to compare the two. Ask, "How many dots would cover the picture of the ladybug? How many bacteria would cover the picture of the ladybug?" Have students use that data to record what fraction of the ladybug a dot is and what fraction a bacterium is. Have them record each answer as a fraction and a decimal.

Wilma Unlimited

Wilma Unlimited, by Kathleen Krull (1996), is a short biography of Wilma Rudolph, an Olympic champion. Wilma contracted polio as a child, which caused paralysis in her left leg. Since she couldn't walk, she hopped. She eventually learned to walk and later, to run. Amazingly, she went from being a disabled child to the world's fastest woman runner, winning three gold medals in the 1960 summer Olympics. Her incredible life provides the opportunity to explore rates for the three paces that Wilma experienced in her lifetime: hopping, walking, and running.

In this investigation, students create tables and graphs to examine the relationships among the three different paces in seconds per meter (not meters per second, as is more common). In other words, students discover how many seconds it takes to cover a given distance in each of the three paces. Each student creates a graph showing all three paces, with meters as the independent variable (recorded on the *x*-axis) and seconds as the dependent variable (recorded on the *y*-axis).

MATERIALS

timer or watch with a second hand, 1 per pair of students

centimeter-squared paper, 1 sheet per student (see Blackline Masters)

Note: You will also need access to a gymnasium, track, sidewalk, or other place where students can measure distance.

Introducing the Investigation

Before conducting this lesson, find a location in or around your school where you can bring the students to try hopping, walking, and running 40-meter distances themselves, such as a track or playground.

To begin the lesson, read *Wilma Unlimited* to the students. When you're done, ask the students to describe the various ways that Wilma was able to get around (hopping, walking, running). Next, ask students to describe how these modes of travel affected the rate that she could travel. Rate is often referred to as distance per time, such as miles per hour, and students will most likely offer this as an explanation first. This activity requires students to look at rate as time per distance, or how much time it takes to go a given distance. Ask students to brainstorm other rate situations, such as words per minute when typing, gum per package, or sheets of paper per ream.

Next, have students gather into pairs and take them to the location you selected previously. Explain to them that one student will hop a 40-meter distance (already measured off by you), while the partner uses a stopwatch to record the time on a sheet of paper. When the first person is done hopping, the two should switch roles; then they should repeat the process for walking and running. When all pairs have completed this task, return to the classroom. Ask students to take their

Figure 30–1: Katie created tables for the data she collected.

40 meters

Hop – 14 sec.

Walk – 24 sec.

Run – 7 sec.

Hop	
Dist.	Time
40 m	14 sec.
30 m	10.5
20 m	7 sec.
10 m	3.5
1 m	.35

Walk	
Dist.	Time
40 m	24 sec.
30 m	18 sec
20 m	12 sec.
10 m	6 sec
1 m	.6

Run	
Dist.	Time
40 m	7 sec.
30 m	5 sec
20 m	3.5 sec
10 m	1.5 sec
1 m	.15

Math and Literature, Grades 6–8

own data and create a table for each pace (with distance in the first column and time in the second). The data in the table should include the time to travel each of the following distances (assuming they moved at a constant rate): 40 meters, 30 meters, 20 meters, 10 meters, 1 meter, and zero meters (see below). Students may use various strategies for figuring the times, for example, finding 20 meters first by finding half of the time it took to move 40 meters.

Distance (in meters)	Time (in seconds)
40	56
30	42
20	28
10	14
1	1.4
0	0

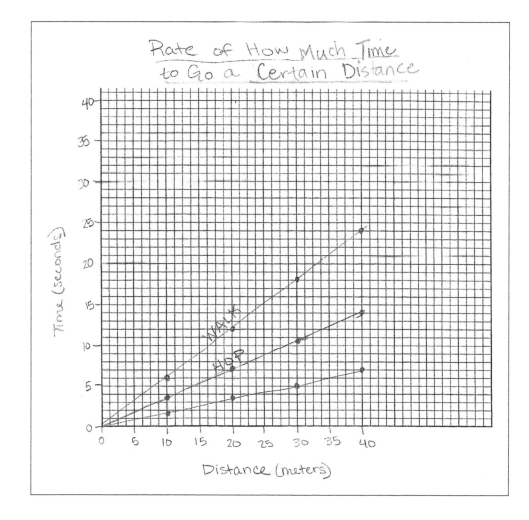

Figure 30-2: Katie created a line graph from the data in the three tables.

When students are finished with their tables, ask them to create graphs for each of the three modes of travel on a sheet of centimeter-squared paper using a different-colored pencil for each pace. Discuss with students how to label the graphs. Distance (in meters) is the independent variable, and therefore should go on the x-axis, and time (in seconds), the dependent variable, should go on the y-axis. They will also have to determine a scale so that all three paces will fit on the graph. Students should plot the ordered pairs from their tables and connect them with a line. Ask students why the data forms a straight line. Students should recognize that the line is straight because the rate was constant. Ask students to explain which pace is the steepest line and why. Ask students to find their rates for each pace in their tables and on their graphs. You can also have pairs exchange graphs and determine each other's rate (seconds per meter) for each of the three paces. (See Figures 30–1 and 30–2 for one student's tables and graph.)

Blackline Masters

Earthshine Record Sheet
Eighteen Flavors Ice-Cream Shapes
The Greedy Triangle Regular Polygon Shapes
Centimeter-Squared Paper
How Much Is a Million? Instructions
How Much Is a Million? Measurement Cards
One Inch Tall Record Sheet
Shapes Worksheet
Important Dates of the *Endurance* Expedition
What's Faster Than a Speeding Cheetah? Record Table
Anno's Hat Tricks Statement Cards
Anno's Hat Tricks Color Cards
My Little Sister Ate One Hare Food Cards
My Little Sister Ate One Hare Record Table
Dot Paper
Millimeter-Squared Paper

Earthshine Record Sheet

Name _____

Prediction	Item	Amount	Cost	Cost/Gallon
	Dragon Blood			

Explain how you converted *one* of the items above into cost per gallon.

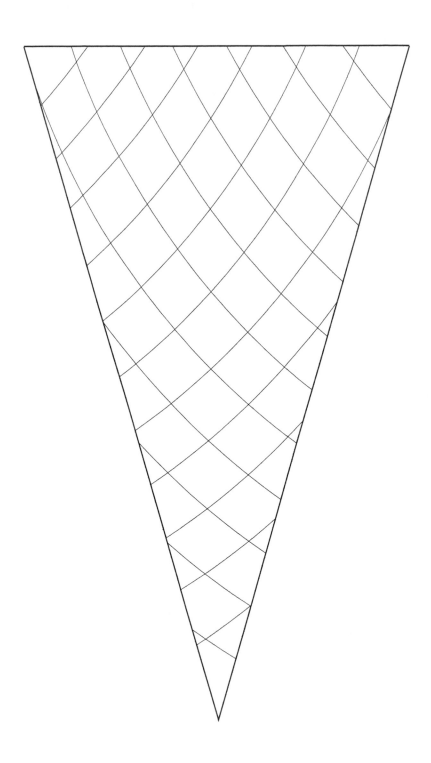

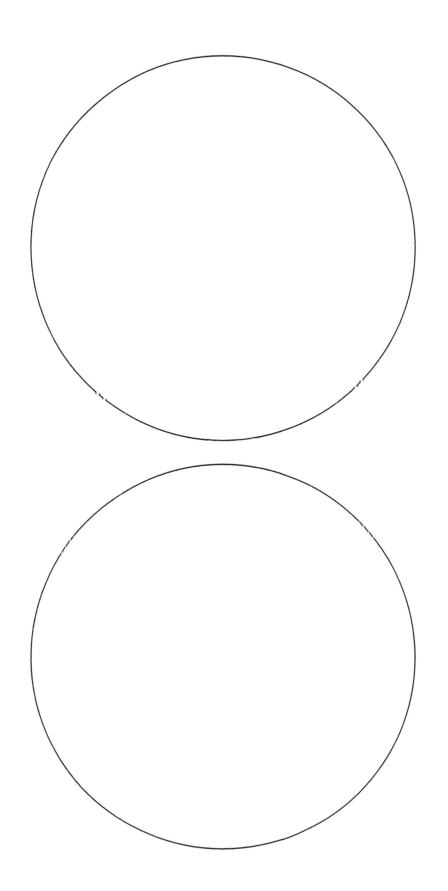

The Greedy Triangle Regular Polygon Shapes

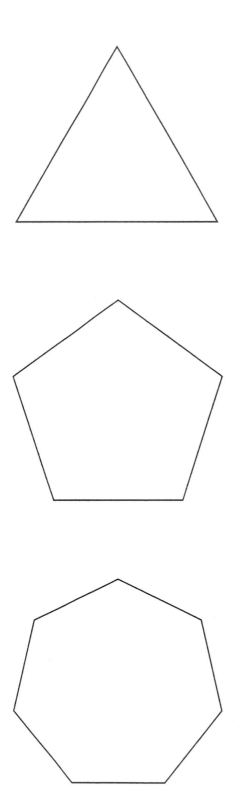

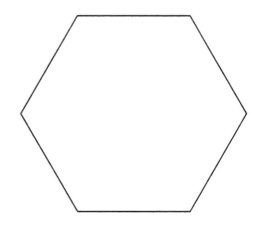

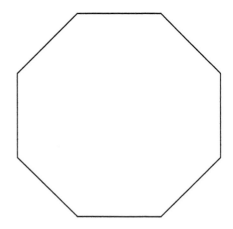

148

From *Math and Literature, Grades 6–8,* by Jennifer M. Bay-Williams and Sherri L. Martinie. © 2004 Math Solutions Publications.

Centimeter-Squared Paper

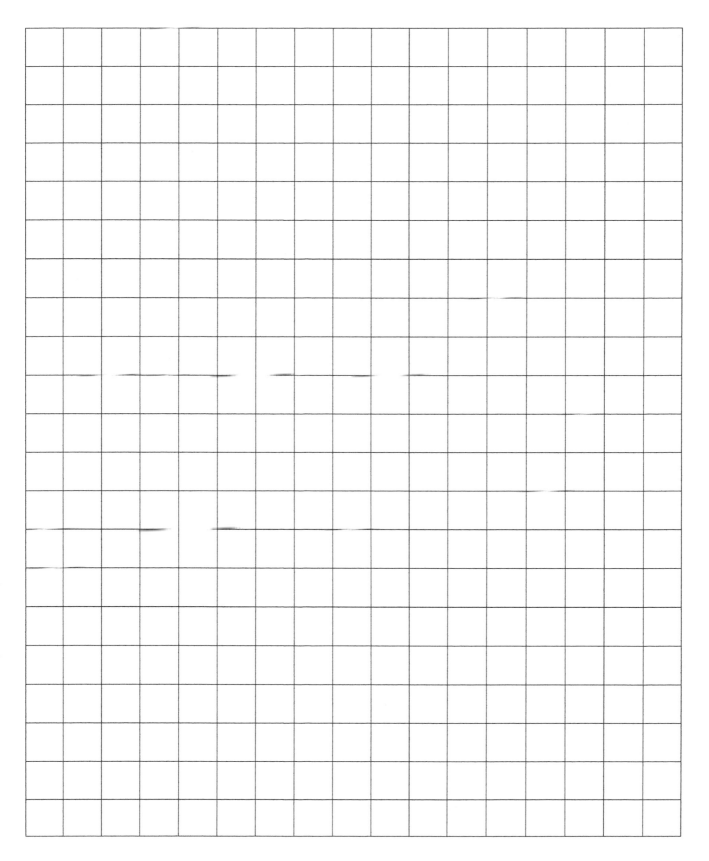

How Much Is a Million? Instructions

With your group, create an illustration of what 1 million looks like. You will be given a card with a type of measurement (e.g., length or area). Your illustration must use that type of measurement to help the rest of us visualize how big 1 million is.

Your final product must:

1. use the measurement you were assigned;

2. use a familiar benchmark as a comparison; and

3. show and explain how you solved the problem.

From *Math and Literature, Grades 6–8*, by Jennifer M. Bay-Williams and Sherri L. Martinie. © 2004 Math Solutions Publications.

Length	Height
Area	Volume
Weight	

One Inch Tall Record Sheet

If you were 1 inch tall, how big would this be . . .

A. Use your 1-inch measuring string (to the nearest eighth of an inch) to find the height of these items in the classroom, assuming they shrank along with you!

B. Your task is to determine if these measurements are correct. Use your measurement from Column A and determine what the length of your desk should be in real life. You *cannot* use a ruler to measure the desk. Do this for each item below and record in Column B.

C. When you have finished with the estimations, use a real yardstick to find the actual measurements and record them in the last column. How accurate were your estimates?

Item	A. String Measurement	B. Estimated Real Measurement	C. Real Measurement
1. Length of your desk			
2. Length of math book			
3. Height of your chair			
4. Width of classroom door			
5. Height of bookshelf/closet door			
6. Width of a window			
7. Length of your pencil			
8. Height of garbage can			
9. Item of your choice:			
10. Item of your choice:			

From *Math and Literature, Grades 6–8*, by Jennifer M. Bay-Williams and Sherri L. Martinie. © 2004 Math Solutions Publications.

Shapes Worksheet

For each of your circles, measure the circumference and the diameter. Then calculate the ratio. Record your measurements and calculations in the table.

Circle Number	Circumference	Diameter	Ratio of C to D
1			
2			
3			
4			
Average			

Explain what you know about the relationship between the circumference and the diameter.

Important Dates of the *Endurance* Expedition

August 8, 1914: *Endurance* departs London for the Southern Hemisphere.

October 1914: *Endurance* arrives in Buenos Aires, Argentina.

October 26, 1914: *Endurance* leaves Buenos Aires for South Georgia Island.

November 5, 1914: *Endurance* lands on South Georgia Island.

December 5, 1914: *Endurance* leaves South Georgia Island for Antarctica.

December 9, 1914: *Endurance* begins to pick its way through ice in the Weddell Sea.

January 19, 1915: *Endurance* becomes trapped in the ice off the coast of Antarctica.

June 22, 1915: The crew celebrates Midwinter's Day on the trapped ship.

October 27, 1915: *Endurance* is crushed by ice and the crew abandons ship.

November 21, 1915: *Endurance* sinks.

April 9, 1916: Boats launch from Antarctica and head to Elephant Island.

April 15, 1916: Boats arrive at Elephant Island.

April 24, 1916: *James Caird* (one of the three boats on the *Endurance*) departs Elephant Island for South Georgia Island.

May 10, 1916: *James Caird* lands at South Georgia Island.

What's Faster Than a Speeding Cheetah? Record Table

Using the speed of each animal or object below, figure out how much time it would take that animal or object to get to the Moon.

At this speed . . .	It would take . . . to get to the Moon.
Ostrich (45 miles per hour)	
Cheetah (70 miles per hour)	
Peregrine Falcon (200 miles per hour)	
Propeller Plane (300 miles per hour)	
Supersonic Jet (1,400 miles per hour)	
Rocket Ship (25,000 miles per hour)	
Meteoroid (150,000 miles per hour)	
Light (186,000 miles per second)	

Explain how you found the answer to *one* of the above problems.

Anno's Hat Tricks Statement Cards

I don't know.	My hat is red.	My hat is white.
I don't know.	My hat is red.	My hat is white.
I don't know.	My hat is red.	My hat is white.
I don't know.	My hat is red.	My hat is white.
I don't know.	My hat is red.	My hat is white.
I don't know.	My hat is red.	My hat is white.
I don't know.	My hat is red.	My hat is white.
I don't know.	My hat is red.	My hat is white.

From *Math and Literature, Grades 6–8*, by Jennifer M. Bay-Williams and Sherri L. Martinie. © 2004 Math Solutions Publications.

RED	RED
RED	WHITE
WHITE	RED
RED	RED
WHITE	WHITE

My Little Sister Ate One Hare Food Cards

Hare	Snake	Snake	Ant	Ant
Ant	Shrew	Shrew	Shrew	Shrew
Bat	Bat	Bat	Bat	Bat
Mouse	Mouse	Mouse	Mouse	Mouse
Mouse	Polliwog	Polliwog	Polliwog	Polliwog
Polliwog	Polliwog	Polliwog	Worm	Worm

From *Math and Literature, Grades 6–8*, by Jennifer M. Bay-Williams and Sherri L. Martinie. © 2004 Math Solutions Publications.

My Little Sister Ate One Hare Food Cards

Worm	Worm	Worm	Worm	Worm
Worm	Lizard	Lizard	Lizard	Lizard
Lizard	Lizard	Lizard	Lizard	Lizard
Pea	Pea	Pea	Pea	Pea
Pea	Pea	Pea	Pea	Pea

My Little Sister Ate One Hare Record Table

	Tallies	Totals	Fraction of Total	Percent of Total	Theoretical Probability (Percent)
Hares					
Snakes					
Ants					
Shrews					
Bats					
Mice					
Polliwogs					
Worms					
Lizards					
Peas					

From *Math and Literature, Grades 6–8*, by Jennifer M. Bay-Williams and Sherri L. Martinie. © 2004 Math Solutions Publications.

Dot Paper

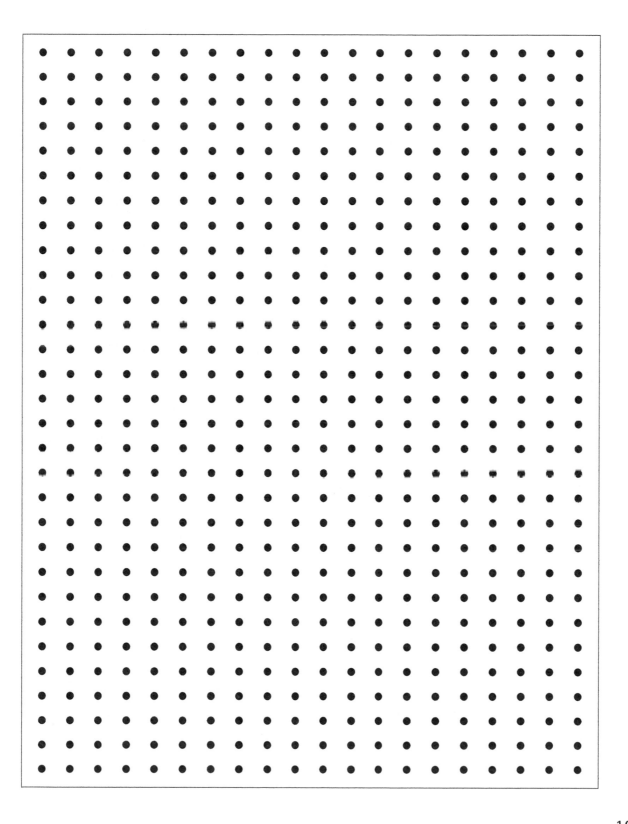

Millimeter-Squared Paper

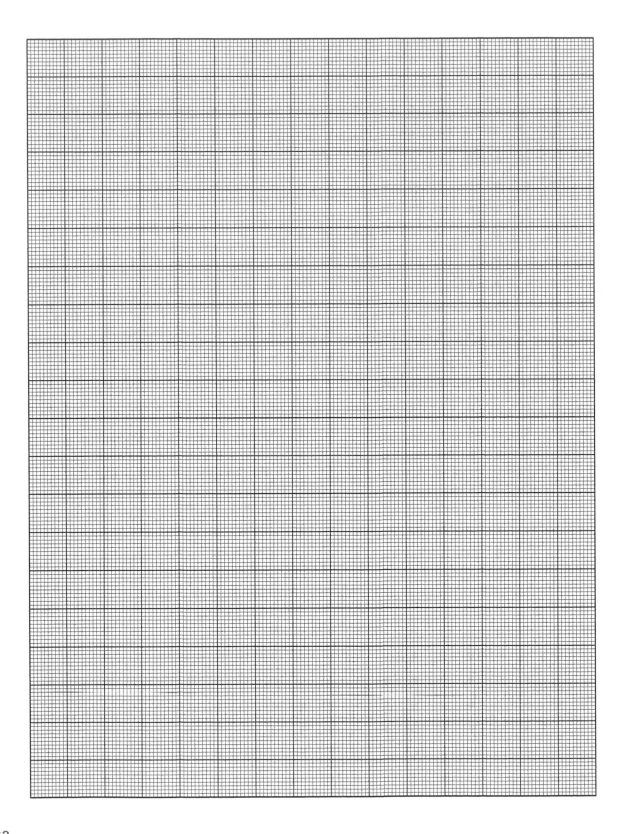

From *Math and Literature, Grades 6–8*, by Jennifer M. Bay-Williams and Sherri L. Martinie. © 2004 Math Solutions Publications.

References

Armstrong, Jennifer. 1998. *Shipwreck at the Bottom of the World: The Extraordinary True Story of Shackleton and the Endurance.* New York: Crown.

Ash, Russell. 1999. *Factastic Book of 1,001 Lists.* New York: DK Publishing.

Briggs, Raymond. 1970. *Jim and the Beanstalk.* New York: Putnam and Grosset.

Burns, Marilyn. 1994. *The Greedy Triangle.* Illus. Gordon Silveria. New York: Scholastic.

———. 1997. *Spaghetti and Meatballs for All! A Mathematical Story.* Illus. Debbie Tilley. New York: Scholastic.

Collier, Mary Jo, and Peter Collier. 1996. *The King's Giraffe.* Illus. Stéphane Poulin. New York: Simon and Schuster.

Grifalconi, Ann. 1986. *The Village of Round and Square Houses.* New York: Little, Brown.

Grossman, Bill. 1996. *My Little Sister Ate One Hare.* Illus. Kevin Hawkes. New York: Crown.

Hobbs, Will. 1996. *Far North.* New York: Avon.

Juster, Norton. 1961/1989. *The Phantom Tollbooth.* Illus. Jules Feiffer. New York: Random House.

Krull, Kathleen. 1996. *Wilma Unlimited: How Wilma Rudolph Became the World's Fastest Woman.* Illus. David Diaz. New York: Harcourt.

Losi, Carol A., with Marilyn Burns. 1997. *The 512 Ants on Sullivan Street.* Illus. Patrick Merrell. New York: Scholastic.

Mosel, Arlene. 1968. *Tikki Tikki Tembo.* Illus. Blair Lent. New York: Henry Holt.

Myller, Rolf. 1962/1990. *How Big Is a Foot?* New York: Dell Yearling.

Nelson, Theresa. 1994. *Earthshine.* New York: Orchard.

Nozaki, Akihiro. 1985. *Anno's Hat Tricks.* Illus. Mitsumasa Anno. New York: Philomel.

Orwell, George. 1946. *Animal Farm.* New York: Signet Classic.

Pinczes, Elinor J. 1993. *One Hundred Hungry Ants.* Illus. Bonnie MacKain. Boston: Houghton Mifflin.

Poe, Edgar Allan. 1983. *The Tell-Tale Heart and Other Writings.* New York: Bantam.

Rowling, J. K. 1999. *Harry Potter and the Sorcerer's Stone.* New York: Scholastic.

Sachar, Louis. 1998. *Holes.* New York: Dell Yearling.

Schwartz, David M. 1985. *How Much Is a Million?* Illus. Steven Kellogg. New York: Mulberry.

Silverstein, Shel. 1974. *Where the Sidewalk Ends.* New York: HarperCollins.

———. 1976. *The Missing Piece.* New York: HarperCollins.

———. 1981. *A Light in the Attic.* New York: HarperCollins.

Taylor, Mildred D. 1991. *Roll of Thunder, Hear My Cry.* New York: Puffin.

Wells, Robert E. 1995. *What's Smaller Than a Pygmy Shrew?* Morton Grove, IL: Albert Whitman.

———. 1997. *What's Faster Than a Speeding Cheetah?* Morton Grove, IL: Albert Whitman.

Wick, Walter. 1997. *A Drop of Water: A Book of Science and Wonder.* New York: Scholastic.

Index